I0114636

The Law
In Quest of Itself

By

LON L. FULLER

THE LAWBOOK EXCHANGE, LTD.
Clark, New Jersey

ISBN 9781584770169 (hardcover)
ISBN 9781616193218 (paperback)

Lawbook Exchange edition 1999, 2012

The quality of this reprint is equivalent to the quality of the original work.

THE LAWBOOK EXCHANGE, LTD.

33 Terminal Avenue
Clark, New Jersey 07066-1321

*Please see our website for a selection of our other publications
and fine facsimile reprints of classic works of legal history:*
www.lawbookexchange.com

Library of Congress Cataloging-in-Publication Data

Fuller, Lon L., 1902-
    The law in quest of itself / by Lon L. Fuller.
        p.   cm.
    Originally published: Boston : Beacon Press, 1966. (Beacon
    series in classics of the law)
    "A series of three lectures provided by the Julius Rosenthal
    Foundation for General Law, and delivered at the Law School of
    Northwestern University at Chicago in April, 1940.
    Includes bibliographical references and index.
    ISBN 1-58477-016-3 (acid-free paper)
        1. Legal positivism. 2. Natural law. 3. Law—Philosophy.
    I. Julius Rosenthal Foundation for General Law.   II. Title.
    III. Series: Beacon series in classics of the law.
    K331.F84   1999
    340'.112—dc21   99-32863
                                                              CIP

Printed in the United States of America on acid-free paper

The Law
In Quest of Itself

By

LON L. FULLER

BEACON PRESS   BOSTON

A series of three lectures provided by the Julius Rosenthal Foundation for General Law, and delivered at the Law School of Northwestern University at Chicago in April, 1940

Copyright 1940 by Northwestern University

First published as a Beacon Paperback in 1966, by arrangement with the author

Published simultaneously in Canada by Saunders of Toronto, Ltd.

Beacon Press books are published under the auspices of the Unitarian Universalist Association

Printed in the United States of America

CONTENTS

Lecture I

•

The Choice Between Natural Law
and Legal Positivism

•

The History of Legal Positivism
from Hobbes to the Analytical Jurists

I

INCLUDED in the many bits of miscellaneous counsel which Hobbes offers the reader of his *Leviathan* is a passage in which he informs him how he should "regulate" his "Trayne of Thoughts." Under this heading he deals with a problem which must have bothered all of us at times, that of knowing what to do "in case our thoughts begin to wander." The cure he prescribes is that we should recall to our minds the object we were seeking to achieve in our thinking —that we should ask ourselves, in other words, what the problem was we were trying to solve. If we adopt this prescription, Hobbes assures us we shall find that our thoughts have been "quickly again reduced into the way." He concludes with a general admonition: ". . . in all your actions, look often upon what you would have, as the thing that directs all your thoughts in the way to attain it."

This advice, which even Hobbes admitted was perhaps "worne out," may seem obvious and com-

LECTURE I

monplace, yet there is no one who stands in greater
need of it than the legal philosopher. No one
more than he runs the risk of forgetting what he
is trying to do. In no field more than his is the
thinker likely to be lured from his goal into by-
paths of his own thought or fall a victim to his
own metaphors and abstractions. It is a field which
requires a very special effort of orientation. It demands not only that we shall philosophize about
the law, but that we shall to some extent philosophize about our own philosophizing to see what
it is we are ultimately aiming at.

Though there are no doubt many permissible
ways of defining the function of legal philosophy,
I think the most useful is that which conceives of
it as attempting to give a profitable and satisfying
direction to the application of human energies in
the law. Viewed in this light, the task of the legal
philosopher is to decide how he and his fellow
lawyers may best spend their professional lives. In
keeping with this pragmatic conception, we may
test the reality of any particular controversy of
legal philosophy by asking: Would the adoption
of the one view or the other affect the way in
which the judge, the lawyer, the law teacher, or

the law student, spends his working day? Tested
by this criterion, some of the issues about which
jurists have most violently disputed reveal themselves as lacking in any real significance for human
affairs. On the other hand, tested by the same
standard, questions which at first glance seem
sterile and verbal may gain a new reality. This is
perhaps the case with the most abstruse seeming
of all jurisprudential disputes—those which relate
to the proper definition of law. Consider, for example, the choice presented by two such conflicting conceptions of law as that which defines it as
the behavior patterns of judges and that which
defines it as reason applied to human relations.
This choice may seem at first to present only an
issue of linguistic proprieties, about which no one
should become unduly excited. Yet if in these
definitions the word "law" means the life work of
the lawyer, it is apparent that something more
vital than a verbal dispute hinges on the choice
between them. Surely the man who conceives his
task as that of reducing the relations of men to a
reasoned harmony will be a different kind of lawyer
from one who regards his task as that of charting
the behavior sequences of certain elderly state offi-

3

cials. And if the lawyer shapes himself by his conception of the law, so also, to the extent of his influence, does he in turn shape the society in which he lives. When this much may be at stake we cannot dismiss a dispute concerning the proper definition of law as a mere logomachy. To do so would be to commit almost as stupid an error as that of denying the reality of a war because the slogans under which it was fought were logically meaningless, or did not present a clear-cut issue between the contending forces. If definitions of law are mere words, they are words which may significantly direct the application of human energies, and to the extent that they do this they cannot be ignored in a legal philosophy which is concerned with realities.

It is with one of these vital problems of choosing between alternative ways of applying our energies in the law that I shall attempt to deal in these lectures. Specifically the problem is that of choosing between two competing directions of legal thought which may be labelled *natural law* and *legal positivism*. Though the way I shall use these terms does no violence, I believe, to their traditional meanings, it may be well, in order to avoid mis-

4

understanding, if I define as accurately as I can
the sense they will bear in these lectures.

By legal positivism I mean that direction of
legal thought which insists on drawing a sharp
distinction between the law *that is* and the law
that ought to be. Where this distinction is taken
it is, of course, for the sake of the law *that is*, and
is intended to purify it by purging it of what
Kelsen calls "wish-law." Generally—though not in-
variably—the positivistic attitude is associated with
a degree of ethical skepticism. Its unavowed basis
will usually be found to rest in a conviction that
while one may significantly describe the law *that
is*, nothing that transcends personal predilection can
be said about the law *that ought to be*.

Natural law, on the other hand, is the view which
denies the possibility of a rigid separation of the
is and the *ought*, and which tolerates a confusion
of them in legal discussion. There are, of course,
many "systems" of natural law. Men have drawn
their criteria of justice and of right law from many
sources: from the nature of things, from the nature
of man, from the nature of God. But what unites
the various schools of natural law, and justifies
bringing them under a common rubric, is the fact

5

that in all of them a certain coalescence of the *is* and the *ought* will be found. Though the natural-law philosopher may admit the authority of the state even to the extent of conceding the validity of enacted law which is obviously "bad" according to his principles, it will be found in the end that he draws no hard and fast line between law and ethics, and that he considers that the "goodness" of his natural law confers on it a kind of reality which may be temporarily eclipsed, but can never be wholly nullified, by the more immediately effective reality of enacted law. So far as the question of ultimate motives is concerned, it is fairly obvious that if the positivist insists on separating the *is* and the *ought* for the sake of the *is*, the natural-law philosopher is attempting to serve the *ought* when he refuses to draw a sharp distinction between it and the *is*.

As I have drawn the issue between these two directions of legal thought, it may seem that choice between them does not present the kind of problem I described at the outset, that of electing between competing ways of applying our energies in the law. If, as an American philosopher has asserted without apparent irony, there exists a "clear distinction between what is in fact law and what on ethical grounds we think ought to be the law,"[1] then is it not our duty simply to acquiesce in that distinction? If we are presented with an alternative of obfuscation or clarity, how can we legitimately refer to the problem as one of choosing between alternative ways of applying ourselves to legal study? If, as the positivist asserts, there are two distinct routes for legal thought, one directed toward the *is* and the other directed toward the *ought*, what possible utility can there be in following the phantom route of natural law, which pretends to lead in both directions at once?

The answer to these doubts lies in the fact that nature does not, as the positivist so often assumes, present us with the *is* and the *ought* in neatly separated parcels. If there is to be a "clear distinction" between them it will have to be brought about by the analytical efforts of the positivist. Such a distinction may serve as the legitimate end of his activities; it cannot serve as his starting point. A rather trivial illustration will suffice to show, I

[1] Cohen, *A Critical Sketch of Legal Philosophy in America*, in 2 LAW, A CENTURY OF PROGRESS (pub. by New York Univ. Press, 1937) 266, 285.

believe, how difficult it is to draw a sharp line between the *is* and the *ought* in any field touched by creative human energies.

If I attempt to retell a funny story which I have heard, the story as I tell it will be the product of two forces: (1) the story as I heard it, the story *as it is* at the time of its first telling; (2) my conception of the point of the story, in other words, my notion of the story *as it ought to be*. As I retell the story I make no attempt to estimate exactly the pressure of these two forces, though it is clear that their respective influences may vary. If the story as I heard it was, in my opinion, badly told, I am guided largely by my conception of the story as it ought to be, though through inertia or imperfect insight I shall probably repeat turns of phrase which have stuck in my memory from the former telling. On the other hand, if I had the story from a master raconteur, I may exert myself to reproduce his exact words, though my own conception of the way the story ought to be told will have to fill in the gaps left by faulty memory. These two forces, then, supplement one another in shaping the story as I tell it. It is a product of the *is* and the *ought* working together. There is no way of measuring the degree to which each contributes to the final result. The two are inextricably interwoven, to the point where we can say that "the story" as an entity really embraces both of them. Indeed, if we look at the story across time, its reality becomes even more complex. The "point" of the story, which furnishes its essential unity, may in the course of retelling be changed. As it is brought out more clearly through the skill of successive tellers it becomes a new point; at some indefinable juncture the story has been so improved that it has become a new story. In a sense, then, the thing we call "the story" is not something that is, but something that becomes; it is not a hard chunk of reality, but a fluid process, which is as much directed by men's creative impulses, by their conception of the story as it ought to be, as it is by the original event which unlocked those impulses. The *ought* here is just as real, as a part of human experience, as the *is*, and the line between the two melts away in the common stream of telling and retelling into which they both flow.

Exactly the same thing may be said of a statute or a decision. It involves two things, a set of words, and an objective sought. This objective may or may not have been happily expressed in the words chosen by the legislator or judge. This objective, like the point of the anecdote, may be perceived dimly or clearly; it may be perceived more clearly by him who reads the statute than by him who drafted it. The statute or decision is not a segment of being, but, like the anecdote, a process of becoming. By being reinterpreted it becomes, by imperceptible degrees, something that it was not originally. The field of possible objectives is filled with overlapping figures, and the attempt to trace out distinctly one of these figures almost inevitably creates a new pattern. By becoming more clearly what it is, the rule of the case becomes what it was previously only trying to be. In this situation to distinguish sharply between the rule as it is, and the rule as it ought to be, is to resort to an abstraction foreign to the raw data which experience offers us.

It is well to be clear concerning the difficulties which confront positivism in its quest for some criterion of the law *that is*, for these difficulties are by no means apparent without reflection. Common sense tells us that there must be a distinction between *a law* and *a good law*, and at first glance positivism seems amply justified in resting its whole case on the self-evident quality of this distinction. But we must remember that those distinctions which seem too obvious to require analysis are often precisely those which will not stand analysis. Common sense tells me that there is a clear distinction between a thing's being a steam engine and its being a good steam engine. Yet if I have a dubious assemblage of wheels, gears, and pistons before me and I ask, "Is this a steam engine?" it is clear that this inquiry overlaps mightily with the question: "Is this a good steam engine?" In the field of purposive human activity, which includes both steam engines and the law, value and being are not two different things, but two aspects of an integral reality.

It will not do, then, for the positivist to say that he only asks us to take a distinction which would be clear were it not that certain forces, united under the black flag of natural law, had an interest in obfuscating it. The adherent of natural law may properly counter this assertion by replying that the "obfuscation" with which he is charged is really the mark of his superior respect for the obscurity of nature and of his refusal to force reality into a dichotomy of his own making. He may argue as the special merit of his view that it releases for more profitable employment energies which would otherwise be dissipated in a fruitless attempt to separate the inseparable. To this the positivist may reply that whatever the difficulties of his self-imposed task may be, the time and effort which it consumes are more usefully employed than if they were expended in vague speculations on what ought to be. With the lines of opposition thus drawn, it is apparent that we are confronted with a problem not of choosing between what we already have and striving after the unattainable, but of choosing between two kinds of striving. It is also apparent that this problem of choice affects everyone whose activities touch the law.

The one most immediately and obviously affected by it is, of course, the judge. For him it means having to decide such questions as whether he shall take as his model in the field of private law Holmes or Cardozo, Eldon or Mansfield. Is his primary duty one of fidelity to the existing law, or has he a more creative role? Assuming that he has impulses toward reform, how shall those impulses express themselves? Shall he, for example, avoid

the "oblique" methods of judicial legislation ex-
coriated by Austin and Bentham, or shall he
accept them as the inevitable concomitants of an
attempt to improve a tradition while transmitting
it? It is obvious that the problem of knowing how
sharply to distinguish the *is* and the *ought* is one
which extends to every branch of his activities,
and affects not only what he does but the way
he does it.

For the lawyer preparing a brief the problem
is that of choosing a point of anchorage for his
argument. Shall he find it in rules of law or in
the purposes back of those rules? Shall he argue
the rights of his client, or the rightness of his
client's case? Shall he place his appeal on a footing
of elementary conceptions of justice, treating the
rules laid down in the texts and cases as a kind of
secondary and corroborative expression of these
conceptions? Or shall he accept the rules themselves as the prime realities in his legal firmament,
and so marshal them that they appear to compel
a decision in favor of his client?

For the professor of law, the problem is not
only how and what he shall teach, but how he
shall spend his working day outside the classroom.

Shall he find his chief satisfaction in the intellectual stimulation which comes from solving what is known as "the neat case"? Or shall he undertake a pervasive inquiry into the ethical foundations of legal rules, knowing that the price of this inquiry will be the disappearance of "the neat case"—for when rules are no longer treated in abstraction from their purposes, they cease to produce those neat antinomies which the lawyer delights to discuss with his colleagues, and the problem which seemed an intriguing test of juristic ingenuity dissolves into a prosaic question of choosing between competing ethical desiderata. What is the legal scholar's duty toward reform? Does he sufficiently prove his progressiveness by a willingness to construct tenable legal theories to support the reforms effected by judges too busy to explain adequately what they are doing, or is his role a more active one? Is it his duty to anticipate the future by giving legal form to emergent ethical values, or is he only a kind of intellectual scavenger whose function it is to clean up the conceptual debris left behind in the advance of the law?

The problem addresses itself finally to the law

student. Shall he take as his ideal instructor a Gray or an Ames? Shall he search out the professor who can expound "the existing law" as of, let us say, 4 P.M., Tuesday, April 2, 1940, and who has all the latest cases at his finger-tips? Or shall his preference be for the man who can impart an insight into the shifting ethical background of the law, a background against which "the law as it is" appears as an accidental configuration without lasting importance? A similar problem of choice confronts him in directing his own studies. The way in which the law student decides these questions transcends in importance its effects on his own career, for, through the subtle pressures he exerts on his instructors to teach him what he thinks he ought to be taught, he exercises an influence on legal education—and indirectly on the law—much greater than he has any conception of.

It would be fatuous for anyone to pretend that he could exercise a wholly independent judgment in solving questions such as those I have been reviewing. Questions of this sort, which affect the fundamental bent of our lives, are largely decided for us. Their solution emerges as a kind of compromise between certain feeble impulses of our own natures and the much more powerful forces of the intellectual and emotional environment in which we live. But if the individual's power of choice can at best be slight, it can scarcely exist at all until he has analyzed the forces which impinge upon him, until he has discovered what kind of intellectual climate it is he lives in. This means, inevitably, a resort to history, for the prevailing temper of an age—its way of orienting human activities, its conceptions of what is important and what is not—are necessarily conditioned by the past. It is for this reason that I propose, as a step toward securing a better understanding of the issue of natural law *versus* legal positivism, to pass briefly in review the chief schools of legal positivism.[2] As the title of these lectures suggests, this review will involve a study of the law's quest for some exclusive hegemony of its own, for some

2 I have also dealt with the issue of positivism *versus* natural law in three recent book reviews. Hall, *Readings in Jurisprudence* (1939) 78 U. OF PA. L. REV. 623; Pound, *The Formative Era of American Law* (1939) 34 ILL. L. REV. 372; Williston on *Contracts* (1939) 18 N. C. L. REV. 1, 13-15. These reviews supplement in certain respects what I have to say in these lectures, particularly as it affects contemporary currents of thought in this country.

Ultima Thule where its existence can be free from the complications of ethics and philosophy. More specifically, my survey of the history of legal positivism will include the imperative theory of Hobbes, the school of analytical jurisprudence represented by Austin and Somló, the so-called Vienna School founded by Hans Kelsen, and that aspect of American legal realism which has concerned itself with defining law.

I shall not include the sociological "positivism" of Comte, Durkheim, and Duguit. This particular kind of positivism implies not the repudiation of natural law but of metaphysical entities like "the state" and "a right." In practice sociological positivism has never insisted on a rigid separation of *is* and *ought,* and for that reason has never been wholly respectable in the eyes of the legal positivists.[3]

Although the historical school founded by Savigny was formerly often referred to as "positivistic," it is not included here. To be sure, this

[3] See BERGBOHM, JURISPRUDENZ UND RECHTSPHILOSOPHIE (1892) 51; Gurvitch, *Droit Naturel ou Droit Positif Intuitif?* (1933) 3 ARCHIVES DE PHILOSOPHIE DU DROIT ET DE SOCIOLOGIE JURIDIQUE 55, 68.

school seems at first glance to satisfy the definition
I have given of positivism. It was in theory opposed to natural law and to the confusion of the
law that is with the law that ought to be. By
attributing law to a single source, the spirit of
the people, it seems to offer a positivistic criterion
for the law that is which could serve to keep it
free from the contamination of ethics. Yet as
Stammler pointed out in an early article,[4] Savigny
and his followers assumed that there could be
such a thing as a "bad rule of law," that is, a
rule of law that did not truly express the spirit
of the people. This "bad law" must, however, ac-
quire its validity as law from some principle
foreign to the theory of the historical school itself.
And if such a principle exists, then the notion
that the law emanates from the spirit of the people
turns out to express, not a criterion of the law
that is, but a particular kind of natural-law standard for the law that ought to be, and the historical
school loses all pretensions to being "positivistic"

4 *Über die Methode der geschichtlichen Rechtstheorie* (1888),
in 1 RECHTSPHILOSOPHISCHE ABHANDLUNGEN (1925) 3. See also
BERGBOHM, JURISPRUDENZ UND RECHTSPHILOSOPHIE (1892) 232
et seq.

in the sense in which I am using the word here.

Our historical survey of positivism could be made more intelligible if we were able to say definitely of each positivist what objective he was pursuing, and what it was that led him to prefer the route of positivism to that of natural law. Unfortunately this is not possible with the later positivists, for by the time we reach them what Vaihinger called "the law of the preponderance of means to end" has begun to operate, and men have lost sight of the purposes of positivism in manipulating its apparatus. When we go back to the man who may be said to be the father of legal positivism, however, this difficulty is not present. With Thomas Hobbes[5] there was no uncertainty or

5 Among Hobbes' writings the work most relevant to our discussion is, of course, LEVIATHAN. (Subsequent references will be to the pagination of Smith's Edition, Oxford Univ. Press, 1909.) See also THE ELEMENTS OF LAW (ed. Tönnies, Cambridge, 1928) and *A Dialogue of the Common Laws*, in 6 WORKS (Molesworth, 1840) 3-160.

A thorough historical treatment of the doctrine of sovereignty—something I make no pretension of offering here —would of course have to include a study of Bodin. I have felt it possible to leave him out of account in these lectures, partly because his positivism was apparently of a very "impure" variety, being more heavily tinctured with natural

ambiguity about the object which he pursued in constructing his theory. It has been said without paradox that he founded legal positivism on a natural-law basis. His argument ran something as follows. If we look over the objectives, material and spiritual, which men may seek to attain, we see at once that one of these objectives—that of peace and order—is a precondition of all the others, and hence is entitled to priority over them. Without a certain degree of peace and order, art, literature, science—even the enjoyment of the grosser

---

law than Hobbes'; and also because his work has not appreciably influenced later writers on legal (as distinguished from political) subjects. See on Bodin, McILWAIN, CONSTITUTIONALISM AND THE CHANGING WORLD (1939) 40-55, and *passim;* and SABINE, A HISTORY OF POLITICAL THEORY (1937) 399 *et seq.* The assertion of Gurvitch [*Droit naturel ou droit positif intuitif?* (1933) 3 ARCHIVES DE PHILOSOPHIE DU DROIT ET DE SOCIOLOGIE JURIDIQUE 55, 59] that Hobbes' view was anticipated by Protagoras seems unjustified by the scanty references to Protagoras' philosophy contained in Plato and Diogenes Laertius. To be sure, the issue of convention *versus* reason is a theme which recurs frequently in Greek philosophy. But what is lacking in Greek thought is the notion of any organ set up to act as a final arbiter of convention. So far as the underlying spirit of Hobbes' philosophy is concerned, Sabine suggests that among the Greeks the Epicureans were probably closest to him. *Op. cit. supra* 132-136.

physical pleasures, are all impossible, and the life of man is "solitary, poore, nasty, brutish, and short."

How are we to obtain this minimum of peace and order, however, in view of the fact that the interests of men tend inevitably to come in conflict, so that in a natural state men are at war with one another? We cannot bring about this condition of peace and order by reasoning with men. Even assuming that men would always follow right reason if it were given, many of the questions of mine and thine which separate men are not immediately susceptible of solution by reasoning. What is therefore needed is some earthly authority which shall have final power to settle these questions, which shall act as a kind of artificial reason to take the place of natural reason in solving these questions. This earthly power we shall call the Sovereign, and the rules it lays down for the settlement of disputes we shall call Law. This Sovereign should in establishing the law follow the precepts of natural reason as far as these will carry it. Unfortunately, however, there is no possible way of guaranteeing that it will do this. Though reason itself dictates many things about the content of the law, there is no way of drawing a hard and fast line between those things which can be settled by reason and those which must be settled by fiat. Therefore to permit men to pass judgment on the commands of the Sovereign in the light of reason would be to invite revolution and disorder. Men ought accordingly to obey even the unreasonable and unjust commands of the Sovereign, for the evils which flow from obedience are less than those which flow from disobedience. Not only must we follow the commands of the Sovereign, but we must refrain from embroidering them with our own conceits. For if it is true that without the sovereign power "every man would be wolf to another," the first step toward making every man a wolf to his fellow is to allow him to interpret the law as he sees fit.

It will be noted that this view—so simple in its essence that it can hardly be called a "theory"— in no way denies that human reason ought to play an important role in shaping the law. It touches only the question of the sanction which this "ought" should carry. Hobbes himself sets up an elaborate series of principles of natural reason which the Sovereign ought to follow, and his

enumeration is in fact more detailed than that of
most modern jurists who champion the notion of
natural law.[6] It is on this basis that Stammler is
justified in classifying him, without explanation or
apology, along with Pufendorf and Grotius as an
exponent of natural law, distinguishing him from
the second of these authors chiefly by his assumption that man's fundamental nature is antisocial.[7]

It will also be noted that Hobbes' conception of
sovereignty is not overburdened with distinctions
and definitions. Where Hobbes becomes compli-
cated and sophistical is not in expounding the
notion of sovereignty, but in justifying it; not on
the positivistic side of his theory, but on the
natural-law side. His attempts to show that the
sovereign power results from a grant running from
the people to the sovereign, and that this grant
must in its very nature be irrevocable, are remark-
able for their laborious ingenuity but for little
else; certainly not for their power to induce con-

---

[6] See especially Chapters 14, 15, 21, 27, and 30 of LEVIATHAN.

[7] RECHTS- UND STAATSTHEORIEN DER NEUZEIT (2d ed. 1925) 15.
See also DEL VECCHIO, LEZIONI DI FILOSOFIA DEL DIRITTO (3d
ed. 1936) 65; BERGBOHM, JURISPRUDENZ UND RECHTSPHILOSO-
PHIE (1892) 164; ROBERTSON, HOBBES (1886) 142.

viction. We shall not concern ourselves with them
here, for they have had no influence on the later
history of legal positivism. The later positivists
have not attempted to prove the need of a sovereign
power; they have assumed it. The problem which
caused Hobbes so much pain they have solved by
ignoring it.

On the other hand, of the numerous difficulties
which have vexed the later exponents of the imperative theory, only one is discussed at any length
by Hobbes. If we define law as the command of
the sovereign, what shall we say of the law laid
down by the judges? Being subject to the King,
or the Protector, they are certainly not sovereigns
in their own right, and if they were, of course the
unity and effectiveness of the legal order would be
destroyed. It would be natural to regard them
as agents of the sovereign, were it not for the fact
that their decisions customarily purport to rest not
upon the sovereign will, but upon independent
sources, chiefly custom and reason. If the judges
are agents, they are agents who habitually talk as
if they were principals. This difficulty Hobbes
solved by a very simple expedient of method which
has been accepted by his followers ever since, and

which consists essentially in disregarding the judges'
talk. The judge may not think he is an agent of
the sovereign, but he is, since the sovereign adopts
the judge's will as his own.[8] What the sovereign
permits, he impliedly commands. The principle
of agency that the act ratified must have been done
by one who purported to act as agent seems not
to apply in the higher field of positivistic jurisprudence.

It has not infrequently been intimated that the
high value which Hobbes put on peace and order
resulted from some streak of cowardice in his character, aggravated perhaps by the disordered times
in which he lived. This interpretation stands in
strange contrast to Hobbes' own combative nature,
so strongly revealed in the polemical writings which
usurped a large portion of his intellectual energies.
If his view had its origin in his personality, I should
prefer to think that it was a reaction against what
he regarded as a disruptive and wasteful impulse
in his own nature. The man who prides himself
on his willingness to do battle, "the man who loves
a good fight," is often the victim of a modesty

[8] Leviathan 213 [143].

which was foreign. to Hobbes. One who feels himself incapable of anything more productive than fighting will naturally experience no sense of the tragic waste involved in dispute. Hobbes was not of this class. He truly expressed his own motives, I think, when he wrote at the end of his *Leviathan* that he hoped that he had in that work sufficiently disposed of the Artificial Body called the State so that he might return to his "interrupted speculation of Bodies Natural." He sought peace for creative work in a world which was filled with combative impulses, including his own. Yet this fact offers us no basis for condemning his view as "escapist." To the extent that his theory expressed an aspect of his own personality, it at the same time expressed a need of civilized men everywhere.

When we pass down to Hobbes' successors, from among whom we may select Austin and Somló as outstanding, we discover that "the imperative theory of law" has undergone an enormous change.[9]

9 See AUSTIN, LECTURES ON JURISPRUDENCE (4th ed. 1879), and SOMLÓ, JURISTISCHE GRUNDLEHRE (2d ed. 1927). (Somló's book, with its extensive bibliographical apparatus, offers an excellent means of access to the whole literature of positivism.) Of course it is impossible for me to attempt to deal ade-

It is now imbedded in such a maze of distinctions and definitions that it is difficult at times to recognize it as deriving from Hobbes' simple and common-sense view. These complications in the theory have, I think, arisen in two different ways.

In the first place, they in part reflect an increased complexity in the structure of the state. The problem which plagued Austin, how to locate the sovereign power in a government of checks and balances and distributed powers, caused Hobbes no concern. He was able to assume, without too much violence to the facts, that the sovereign power in

---

quately here with the whole school of "analytical jurisprudence." See Pound, *The Progress of the Law, Analytical Jurisprudence, 1914-1927* (1927) 41 HARV. L. REV. 174; Pound, *Fifty Years of Jurisprudence* (1937-1938) 50 HARV. L. REV. 557, 51 HARV. L. REV. 444, 777; Kocourek, *The Century of Analytic Jurisprudence since John Austin,* printed in 2 LAW, A CENTURY OF PROGRESS (pub. by New York Univ. Press, 1937) 195.

One of the most curious books in the history of legal positivism is BERGBOHM, JURISPRUDENZ UND RECHTSPHILOSOPHIE (1892). In this work Bergbohm attempted to show that all of the supposedly positivistic theories of his day were in fact heavily infected with natural-law elements. In a projected second volume he planned to lay down definite criteria of positivism which would remedy this situation and completely exclude natural law from legal thinking. The second volume never appeared.

England would be lodged in a single man, either a King or a Protector. As government became more complex, the concept of sovereign power as a unifying force became more difficult to maintain, since it could no longer derive its unity from its seat in a single human being. An increase in the complexity of the governmental structure to which it related was bound to produce complications in the theory itself.

In the second place—and this is, to my mind, the less obvious but more important factor—what Hobbes viewed as an ethical desideratum, to be achieved with as close an approximation as human affairs permit, was viewed by his successors as something existing independently of the objects it was intended to accomplish. There is, to be sure, the question just what kind of "reality" the later positivists attributed to their sovereign. But whether they regarded it as a datum of nature, or only as a kind of postulated reality with an inner logic of its own like the plot of a play, their sovereign was something to be described, not, as with Hobbes, a program to be carried out. In thus cutting the theory of sovereignty loose from its natural-law roots they paved the way for the subtle and futile discussions which surround later positivist theories.

In attempting a summary of the theory of sovereignty in the form it assumed with the analytical jurists, I shall not undertake a comparison of the views of different authors. What is necessary for our present purposes is a survey of the kinds of questions which have caused embarrassment to Hobbes' successors, and a brief indication of the methods employed in answering them. The similarity of these questions to certain problems of theology is readily apparent, and will be referred to later. I shall try to state the position of the analytical jurists as sympathetically as possible. If their solutions often seem verbal and formal, we must remember that this is not because they preferred solutions of that kind, but because that was the only sort of solution open to them in view of the questions they thought had to be answered. We must judge their achievements in the light of the objectives they sought.

As I have already pointed out, one problem, which we may call that of the *Little Sovereign,* had already been disposed of by Hobbes. This was solved by saying that the man who looked like a Little Sovereign—the judge, let us say—was, in the

eyes of analytical jurisprudence, only an agent of
the Big Sovereign.[10] That this construction of the
judge's position was contrary to his own understanding of it was quite immaterial, because if his
own understanding were adopted it would destroy
the unity of the legal order, which is, in turn, an
essential assumption if we are to retain any criterion
of the law *that is*. Nor are all of those who influence the growth of the law to be admitted even to
the rank of Vice-Sovereign. Text-writers and pro-
fessors, for example, help to shape the law, but
they are not accorded the position of agents of the
sovereign. They are merely persons whose opin-
ions may influence the sovereign or its agents.[11]
That a prediction of the way this influence will
work may rest on a more secure factual basis than a
similar prediction concerning a statute is, of course,
immaterial. We are interested not in the forces
which actually shape men's conduct, but in a legal
construction which reduces those forces to juristic
coherence.

The question, how is the sovereign power to be

10 AUSTIN, *op. cit.* 104; SOMLÓ, *op. cit.* §106.

11 AUSTIN, *op. cit., Lecture XXX;* SOMLÓ, *op. cit.* §106, p. 359;
HOBBES, LEVIATHAN 212 [143].

located in a given society? was answered so satis-
factorily by Austin that the later positivists have
generally accepted his answer without cavil. That
answer was, in brief, to say that the sovereign is
that person or group of persons which society is in
the habit of obeying.[12] It is clear that this conception rests the legal order ultimately on custom,
since the sovereign is, under this view, merely the
beneficiary of a custom of obedience, and the secur-
ity of his position will depend upon the strength
of the custom supporting it.[13] It is equally obvious

---

[12] AUSTIN, *op. cit.* 226 *et seq.;* SOMLÓ, *op. cit.* §29.

[13] Del Vecchio goes a step further and penetrates not only
behind "the sovereign," but also behind the "habit of obedience" which makes the sovereign. He argues that the most
enduring reality in the whole complex of factors which create
"the law" lies in human reason, since whether a given system
of law will receive general acceptance—whether it will en-
gender the requisite habit of obedience—depends ultimately
on the appeal it makes to human reason. *Il Problema delle
Fonti del Diritto positivo* (1934) 14 RIVISTA INTERNAZIONALE
DI FILOSOFIA DEL DIRITTO 184.

Cf., "Turn now to that faction of the positivistic party
which has all law take its origin exclusively in and through
the state, and which regards the statute as the only true
form of law. Now you seem to be on solid ground; here at
least a man knows where he stands. You are wrong! Pursue
your inquiry a little farther, go beyond the notion of the

that in reality the role of custom is not limited to
determining the sovereign power, but that the content of the law itself, and the allocation of powers
among the sovereign's agents, are also in large part
determined by custom. It is furthermore clear that
it may be custom rather than the sovereign power
which furnishes the basic stability of a society, for
as Portalis observed, "L'expérience prouve que les
hommes changent plus facilement de domination
que de lois."[14] For Austin and his followers, however, these effects of custom are mere factual realities without jurisprudential significance. In the
eyes of analytical jurisprudence custom acts *ex pro-
prio vigore* only in establishing the sovereign; any
other effects it may have exist only by the tolerance
of the sovereign and are therefore by implication
in accordance with his assumed commands.

---

state, and you will find yourself right where you started. All
the things against whose arrogated law-giving power you
were once so earnestly warned are back on the scene again:
'the nature of man', 'the natural right of the stronger'—the
same 'peaceful order' founded on 'reason.' . . . You've spoiled
it all by asking too many questions." BERGBOHM, JURIS-
PRUDENZ UND RECHTSPHILOSOPHIE (1892) 116-117.

14 *Discours Préliminaire*, in 1 LOCRÉ, LA LÉGISLATION DE LA
FRANCE (1827) 244, 251.

It follows from this that if occasionally certain commands of the sovereign are ignored, if particular laws are in practice disobeyed with impunity, this does not destroy their character as laws.[15] If it did, our test for the law *that is* would be lost. We could no longer inquire whether the particular rule was commanded, expressly or impliedly, by the sovereign, but would have to inquire instead to what degree the particular rule managed to get itself realized in the affairs of men. Since this is obviously a matter of degree, we would have forfeited our test of the law *that is* and would have opened a great door to contamination from the law that merely ought to be.

The degree to which particular laws are enforced and obeyed is immaterial unless disobedience reaches a point which compels us to say that the sovereign which issues these laws no longer enjoys the obedience of the bulk of society in the generality of cases. In that event we are either in a condition of anarchy or—and this is more usual— a new sovereign power has emerged.[16] It has been

15 Somló, *op. cit.* §35.

16 Austin, *op. cit.* 230-240; Somló, *op. cit.* §§31-32, §§39-40, §95.

said that nature makes no leaps; it may be said of Austin's school that it never moves except by leaping. It recognizes big revolutions, but not little ones. It recognizes changes in an abstract thing called the sovereign, but not in the fabric of men's daily lives. It is clear why this should be so. Basically the quest of positivism is for some test which will designate plainly the law *that is* and distinguish it from the law that is merely becoming or merely ought to be. This test is found by Austin and his school in the concept of the sovereign. This concept cannot possibly perform its function unless it has permanence and unity, unless it can absorb and survive the little revolutions which go on all the time.[17]

More embarrassing for the positivists than the points just discussed is a set of questions which arise out of what we may call *The Problem of the Inconsiderate Sovereign.* The concept of sovereignty is intended to introduce unity into the legal order

[17] "Stünde hinter ihnen [i.e., these minor changes] nicht auch ein relativ fester Kern, so könnte ja von einem Rechte und einem Staate überhaupt nicht gesprochen werden." Somló, *op. cit.* p. 315.

and make positivism possible. If our actual sovereign is what we may call a considerate sovereign he will refrain from doing anything which would impair his usefulness for analytical jurisprudence. He will, first of all, treat himself as legally omnipotent, because if there are any legal limitations on his power we shall have to call in some undesignated third party to act as an arbiter over these limitations and the door will be left ajar for an invasion from the juristic underworld of natural law. For the same reason, our considerate sovereign will not issue contradictory commands, for if he does we might be tempted to take into account considerations of what ought to be in deciding which of his commands to follow. Again, if he is especially considerate, he will see to it that his commands cover the whole field of possible dispute, for if there are gaps in the law, who is to fill the gaps, and how?

But suppose our actual sovereign turns out to be inconsiderate of the demands of legal positivism?[18] Suppose, as a first example, he declares that

[18] The difficulties of the task of forcing the fact of government into the jurisprudential mold of sovereignty seem at

his powers are legally limited? Analytical jurisprudence has two ways of dealing with this infrac-
tion of juristic principle. If there is someone in
sight who can take over his functions, the recalci-
trant sovereign is simply demoted.[19] If the legislature decrees that its laws once passed can be
changed only by a two-thirds vote of the populace,
then we may declare that "the real sovereign power" is located in two-thirds of the people, and the
legislature is only an agent of this higher power.
If there is no other power capable of taking over
the duties of our original sovereign, the situation
is more embarrassing. There is then left only one
step, and that a bold one. That is to declare that
these self-imposed limitations are invalid. Our
sovereign is so powerful that he lacks the power
to limit his own power.[20]

---

times to become oppressive for Somló. In one place he
declares, "Es ist keine geringe Aufgabe, die Sprüche des
Rechtsmachtsorakels zu entziffern, zu deuten und in die klare
Form eines Systems zu giessen." *Op. cit.* p. 17.

[19] See the references in notes 12 and 16 *supra*.

[20] AUSTIN, *op. cit., Lecture VI*, espc. at 254, 264, 270-298.
Somló considers that the sovereign can promise as well as
command, but the obligation imposed by the sovereign's

As to contradictory commands, we shall resolve all doubts in favor of assuming that our sovereign is conscious of his duties to jurisprudence, and that what appears as a contradiction is only apparently so. We are, naturally, cut off from this course if the sovereign himself declares that his commands are or may be contradictory. In that case we are forced again to say that the sovereign is simply wrong; in the eyes of analytical jurisprudence he cannot contradict himself.[21] This should not be

---

promise rests entirely on what Austin called "positive morality"; "legally" the sovereign may withdraw his promise at any time. *Op. cit.* §94 and §104.

" . . . the Bodin-Hobbes-Austin proposition, that sovereign power is incapable of legal limitation, while often denied, is an inescapable proposition of logical truth. There can be nothing more ultimate than ultimateness." Kocourek, *op. cit. supra,* note 9, 200. *Cf.,* " . . . the right to make binding obligations is a competence attaching to sovereignty." Hughes, C. J., in Perry v. United States, 294 U. S. 330, 353 (1935).

21 "The proposition that all the expressions of the highest legal power must be construed into a consistent system of legal rules follows from the nature of law itself. It is therefore inescapable. It cannot be affected by possible provisions of the law to the effect that the expressions of the sovereign must not be interpreted, or that each expression of the legislator must be considered in isolation. It cannot even be abrogated by an express rule that contradictions of

mistaken for a *legal* limit on his powers; his powers remain legally without limit but are subject only to certain jurisprudential restrictions. Neither should these limits on the sovereign's powers be regarded as deriving from natural law, for natural law has to do with the Good Life, while these restrictions proceed from certain ethically indifferent requirements of juristic theory.

The problem of gaps in the law is perhaps the most difficult of all. Legal positivism certainly has an interest in sealing up as many gaps as it can in the system of positive law, for every gap represents a possible point of entry for natural law and ethics. One solution for this problem is to say that there really are no gaps in the law because what the sovereign has not forbidden he impliedly permits. Accordingly, if the plaintiff cannot bring his case

---

the legislator are not to be construed away." SOMLÓ, *op. cit.* 383. See also HOHFELD, FUNDAMENTAL LEGAL CONCEPTIONS (1923) 136. Though Kelsen dispenses with the notion of the sovereign, he also postulates the impossibility of conflicts inside a single legal order. REINE RECHTSLEHRE (1934) 84-89. He explains that if such conflicts were permitted, "dann wäre es um die Einheit der Rechtsordnung geschehen." One might add that legal positivism would also be visited with the same extinction.

within the existing system of constraints set up by
the sovereign, we must enter judgment for the
defendant, and this judgment is in effect directed
by an implied command of the sovereign. This
is the theory of the plenitude of the existing legal
order in its most extreme and repressive form.[22]
Generally legal positivism, not wishing to be ac-
cused of blocking the growth of judge-made law,
has solved the problem of gaps in the law in a
more abstract and less inhibitive manner. Though
there may be no rule in advance for the particular
case, there is a judicial machinery ready to handle
the case. The judge who decides the case is the
authorized agent of the sovereign; his commands
are the commands of the sovereign. Accordingly,
there really are no gaps in the law, since the unprovided-for case is actually provided for; the sovereign
decrees in advance that in the case of "novel impression" the rule to be applied shall be that which

---

[22] See BERGBOHM, JURISPRUDENZ UND RECHTSPHILOSOPHIE (1892)
373; and the writers discussed in SOMLÓ, *op. cit.* §115. Hobbes'
view was that in the absence of more explicit direction the
sovereign should be considered as impliedly ordering the
judge to decide the case according to the "law of nature."
LEVIATHAN 209 [141].

his agent, the judge, considers proper.[23] It is again immaterial that this is not the way the judge himself views the thing. That he refuses to decide the case because there is in his opinion "no law" governing it, does not establish the existence of a gap in the law, because from the standpoint of analytical jurisprudence a decision for the defendant is as much a decision of law as a decision for the plaintiff.[24] The judge makes law even when

[23] SOMLÓ, op. cit. §117. In solving the problem of what he calls "technical gaps" in the law, Kelsen arrives at substantially the same solution, though of course without introducing the notion of sovereignty. REINE RECHTSLEHRE (1934) §§40-41. Both Somló and Kelsen consider that the supposed problem of "gaps in the law" has been largely imagined into existence, for political reasons, by the adherents of natural law. Somló likens these jurists to the hungry fellow in Mark Twain's story who ate a shoe and, on being asked which part he liked best, replied, "The holes." What the partisans of the law of nature like best about the positive law, according to Somló, is its holes, and they naturally tend to exaggerate their extent and importance. SOMLÓ, op. cit. p. 410.

[24] KELSEN, REINE RECHTSLEHRE (1934) §40; Goble, Affirmative and Negative Legal Relations (1922) 4 ILL. L. Q. 94, 98; (1919) 28 YALE L. J. 387, 391 (a Case Comment by Professor Cook). For critical comment on this view see Pound, Fifty Years of Jurisprudence (1937) 50 HARV. L. REV. 557, 574, n. 81; and Fuller, Legal Fictions (1931) 25 ILL. L. REV. 887, 892, n. 208.

he states that he is refusing to make it, and the law which he thus makes is by adoption that of the sovereign. This solution may seem a trifle verbal, but at least it maintains the principle of positivism formally intact.

Analytical jurisprudence approaches theology most closely perhaps in dealing with the interrelations of its own trinity, which consists of the Law, the State, and the Sovereign. Are these three things, or three aspects of the same thing? Is the State the personification of the Law, or is the Law an instrument of the State? Is the State something set up by the Sovereign, or is the Sovereign merely the personification of the power of the State? I shall not attempt to discuss these finer points of political theory here. The fact that they have been solemnly disputed by intelligent men in the twentieth century is evidence enough, however, of the danger of attempting to deal with conceptual entities without reference to the ends they are intended to serve, and is another exemplification of Nietzsche's trenchant dictum that the commonest stupidity consists in forgetting what one is trying to do.

THE LAW IN QUEST OF ITSELF

Lecture II

•

Two Modern Forms of Legal Positivism

•

Legal Realism

•

The Pure Theory of Law of the Vienna School

•

Jurisprudence and Theology

•

The Ends Served by Legal Positivism

II

NO MORE profound study of the school of
the analytical jurists than that involved in
the brief review just concluded is needed, I
think, to disclose the basic difficulty with their
theory, to uncover the big problem from which
all their little problems stem. This basic difficulty
lies in the notion of sovereignty itself. It is not
that the function of the sovereign is obscure. He,
or it, is intended to introduce into governmental
phenomena a unifying principle which will make
possible at least a formal answer to the question,
"What is the law?" The answer is, of course, "That
which the sovereign adopts as its will." There is,
then, no difficulty in seeing what the sovereign *does*.
It makes legal positivism possible. The real difficulty
lies in knowing what the sovereign *is*. Is it a real
thing, a datum of nature existing apart from men's
thinking? Or is it merely a way of viewing the
world of possible legal phenomena? Is it an actual-
ity, or a metaphor? A thing, or a point of view?

45

This was a question about which Austin was never able entirely to make up his mind, and as a result his whole book is tinctured with a pervasive ambiguity. On the one hand, by insisting repeatedly that the sovereign must be a *"determinate"* person or group of persons he seems to indicate that his sovereign is something real.[1] On the other hand, there are numerous passages in his work which imply an admission that his whole theory represents only a juristic construction of the facts, an interpretation rather than a description. This side of his theory is reinforced by his insistence that the sovereign can act legally only in its corporate capacity.[2] He seems throughout to waver between an attempt to describe the forces which actually run society, and an attempt to construct in somewhat figurative language a constitutional theory of the legal order.

We may say of modern positivistic theories that they diverge along the two sides of Austin's ambiguity. On the one hand, what may be called the "realist" view is represented by numerous Ameri-

[1] 1 JURISPRUDENCE 189 *et seq.*

[2] *Id.* 194.

can writers[3] and such Europeans as Kornfeld[4] and Ehrlich.[5] These men represent that direction of legal positivism which seeks to anchor itself in some datum of nature, which considers that the law's quest of itself can end successfully only if it terminates in some tangible external reality. At the opposite pole is the so-called Vienna School, founded by Hans Kelsen.[6] Though there is no evidence that Kelsen was actually influenced by Austin's book in constructing his theory, those familiar with Austin may profitably view Kelsen's work as a development of Austin's theory in the direction opposite to that taken by the realists. With Kelsen legal positivism is founded not on an objective reality, but on a methodological premise; not on a fact, but on an assumption.

In undertaking first a brief survey of the realist trend in modern legal positivism, I shall not at-

[3] See notes 7-11 *infra.*

[4] SOZIALE MACHTVERHÄLTNISSE (1911); ALLGEMEINE RECHTSLE- HRE UND JURISPRUDENZ (1920).

[5] GRUNDLEGUNG DER SOZIOLOGIE DES RECHTS (1913), trans. by Moll, FUNDAMENTAL PRINCIPLES OF THE SOCIOLOGY OF LAW (1936); DIE JURISTISCHE LOGIK (2d ed. 1925).

[6] See note 24 *infra.*

tempt to discuss in detail the views of particular writers. What we are interested in primarily is a direction of thought; how far particular thinkers have traveled in that direction is a secondary matter.

A distinct turn. in the realist direction is discernible in the first systematic exposition of legal positivism which appeared in this country, that is, in Gray's *Nature and Sources of the Law,* published in 1909 when the author was seventy years old.[7] Gray, who acknowledges that his original inspiration came from Austin, assumed that Austin intended his sovereign to be something real, and he felt that he had sufficiently refuted Austin's theory by showing that the real rulers of society cannot be a "determinate" group of persons, but are in fact a shifting and anonymous body. Indeed, if we look at government as a whole it is hard to see any unity other than the artificial and imported unity implied by the conception of the state. On the other hand, if we narrow our field of inquiry, and concern ourselves with the problem, what is law? as it arises in the practice of the attorney,

[7] Second edition edited by Roland Gray (1921).

48

the search for some unifying principle is not so hopeless. We are here in a position to recapture some of the simplicity of Hobbes' theory. Just as Hobbes was able to assume, without unduly straining the facts, that the King or Protector was sovereign in the political field, so Gray was able to assume that in the practice of the attorney the judge was sovereign. Here a concentration of actual power in a definite human being made possible a definition of law that was at once useful and "realistic." Gray was therefore able to define law as the rules laid down by the courts. According to this view, even a statute was not law, but only a possible source of law, until it had been interpreted and applied by the courts. It is the judge who now stands in the place of Hobbes' personal sovereign, and Gray, like Hobbes, seems to have had in mind primarily a real flesh and blood creature and not a juristic abstraction.

Though Gray's theory represented, as against Austin, a decided step in the direction of realism, it fell short of its mark, in at least two respects. In the first place, though Gray repudiated Austin's sovereign as a mere ghostly construct, and substituted his judge, presumably because he was

something real, there remain traces even in Gray
of the wavering which ran through Austin's theory.
Even with Gray the factual concentration of power
was not wholly adequate to the juristic need for a
unified legal order, and he too had his difficulties
with the inconsiderate sovereign. What shall we
say, for example, of the situation where the judges
are at odds with one another, where they lay down
different rules for the same case? In such a situation Gray concluded that the law must consist in
the rules laid down by a majority of the Supreme
Court.[8] Here, pretty obviously, we have a depart-

---

[8] THE NATURE AND SOURCES OF THE LAW (2d ed. 1921) 117.
The question of "the unity of the legal order" has not preoccupied the later American realists. As a matter of fact,
the definition of law as official behavior, if taken seriously,
would seem to remove the whole subject to a plane of discussion on which the problem of "legal unity" would cease
to be relevant. However, in an article published in 1923,
Professor Cook apparently accepted as a necessary presupposition of legal thinking the existence of a unified legal
order. Only such an assumption could justify the assertion that
conflicting rights are impossible within a single legal system,
and that where equity will restrain the enforcement of a
legal right, the legal right is not actually "valid." *Equitable
Defenses* (1923) 32 YALE L. J. 645, 649. Llewellyn [in *A Realistic Jurisprudence—The Next Step* (1930) 30 COL. L. REV.
431, 455] and Ehrlich [in DIE JURISTISCHE LOGIK (2d ed. 1925)

ure from complete "realism." Gray is no longer treating his judges as mere men, who can differ, but as links in a juristic hierarchy where all inconsistencies must be resolved in a higher instance. It is no longer the individual judge who is taking the place of Austin's sovereign, but a corporate entity which begins to take on some of the complexities of the notion of the King in Parliament.

Gray's theory fell short of the realist ideal in a second respect when, ignoring a lead which Holmes had thrown out twelve years before, he defined law not as the rules *acted on* by courts but as the rules "laid down" by courts. It is clear that the rules judges talk about, or "lay down," are not always the same as the rules on which they act, if for no other reason than because they, like the rest of us, often have difficulty in articulating the bases of their actions.

Since Gray, the general tendency of legal posi-

121-147] have treated the conception of the unity of the law as a "fiction." Ehrlich refers specifically to the conflict of equity and the common law in England as proof of the fictitious character of this notion.

tivism in this country has been in the direction of increasing "realism," that is, in pressing the search for some criterion of the existing law into the field of fact, and out of the field of concept and interpretation. A suggestion first made by Holmes in 1897,[9] and developed systematically by Bingham in 1912,[10] has today been taken up by a sufficient number of writers so that we may properly speak of a "realist school."[11] This view has sought its criterion of positivism not in what judges *say*, but in what they *do*. According to this view, a rule of

[9] See *The Path of the Law* (1897), in COLLECTED LEGAL PAPERS (1920) 167.

[10] *What is the Law?* (1912) 11 MICH. L. REV. 1, 109.

[11] The most important expositions of the realist conception of law (other than those of Holmes and Bingham) are probably the following: Cook, *The Logical and Legal Bases of the Conflict of Laws* (1924) 33 YALE L. J. 457; Llewellyn, *A Realistic Jurisprudence—The Next Step* (1930) 30 COL. L. REV. 431; FRANK, LAW AND THE MODERN MIND (1930). For a more extensive bibliography of the realist movement see Llewellyn, *Some Realism about Realism* (1931) 44 HARV. L. REV. 1222, 1257-1259. It should be noted, however, that only a few of the "realists" listed by Llewellyn have concerned themselves with the problem of defining law, and in the case of most of those listed it can scarcely be said that they have taken any definite stand on the issue of natural law *versus* positivism.

law is a generalization about the way judges act; or, as it has been phrased, the law consists in patterns of judicial behavior. These patterns of behavior are the object of the lawyer's study, just as the behavior of atoms constitutes a field of research for the physicist.

Though, as I have just indicated, the realist conception of law has always placed primary emphasis on *judicial* behavior, the question has been raised whether it ought not to be extended to include a broader field of human conduct. For example, why should we stop with judges and exclude commissioners?[12] And for that matter, what of officials whose duties are even further removed from those of a judge, like the sheriff and the sanitary inspector? They too "behave" in ways that are important to the rest of us, and they too have their rules that they talk about and their rules that they act on. Should we not, then, extend our definition of law to embrace the behavior of all

[12] In commenting on Holmes' definition of law as "the prophecies of what courts will do in fact," Cook writes, "The word 'courts' should include some other more or less similar officials." *The Logical and Legal Bases of the Conflict of Laws* (1924) 33 YALE L. J. 457, 465, n. 31.

state officials?[18] Can we stop even there? After
all, the distinction between "officials" and "laymen" does not rest upon an observable fact, like
the wearing of a badge or a robe, but upon a
normative order, upon a system of rules existing
antecedently to men's behavior under them.[14] Yet
this assumed normative order, which tells us who
is an official, is exactly the kind of thing that realism attempts to eliminate from the study of the

[18] "The emphasis in this book on the conduct of judges is
admittedly artificial. Lawyers and their clients are vitally
concerned with the ways of all governmental officials. . . . "
FRANK, LAW AND THE MODERN MIND 47, note. See also the
heading *Administrative Action as Law* in Llewellyn, *A Realistic Jurisprudence,* 30 COL. L. REV. 431, 455.

[14] " . . . why is Prof. Cook interested in what the *judge*
will do, and not in what Mr. X will write about the case?
Because the judge is the *competent organ* to give the decision, and he is the competent organ only on account of a
legal norm. How can Prof. Cook, as a physicist, tell us that
a man is a *judge?* The doctor always will find only a biological, physiological unit belonging to the *genus homo
sapiens,* but never a judge. . . . In a word, if Prof. Cook
tells us that he is interested in what the *judge* will do, he
introduces, in a disguised manner, the whole normativity
of the law, because it is the *law* alone which makes a man
a judge." Kunz, *The "Vienna School" and International Law*
(1934) 11 N. Y. U. L. Q. REV. 370, 377, n. 13.

law. If, therefore, we are to be completely realistic must we not extend our definition of law to include the behavior of laymen? As a matter of fact, there are to be found in the literature some expressions tending to make just such an extension of the concept of law, and in these the realist view approaches perilously close to the proposition that the law is the way everyone behaves.[15]

It is sometimes supposed that this definition of law in terms of human conduct, as distinguished from meanings and intentions, is merely a juristic offshoot of the behavioristic movement in modern psychology. I believe that this view overestimates the influence of behaviorism, and that the psychology involved in the realist view is largely indigenous to the soil of legal positivism. We must recall what legal positivism sets out to do. Its object is to develop a criterion which will enable us to distinguish between those ideas or meanings which are only trying to become law and those

15 See the heading *Laymen's Behavior as a Part of Law* in Llewellyn, *A Realistic Jurisprudence*, 30 COL. L. REV. 431, 457; and Moore, *Rational Basis of Legal Institutions* (1923) 23 COL. L. REV. 609.

which have succeeded—to set up a kind of finish-
ing line, as it were. With Austin the test was,
roughly, "Those ideas and meanings have become
law which have been approved as such by the
sovereign." This test is rejected by the realists
because Austin's sovereign is a purely imaginary
creature. Gray tried to tie the law down to the
expressed meanings of the individual judge. Obviously, however, the notion that the law lies in
the meanings of particular individuals in particular situations can offer no definite criterion of
positivism, and no assurance against a relativistic
subjectivism in which the distinction between what
is and what ought to be is lost. Viewed "objectively" the meaning of the individual is subject
to reinterpretation by the observer; viewed "sub-
jectively" it is a fleeting posture of the mind which
can never be wholly recaptured. Since "meanings"
will not do, our search for objectivity presses us
on to "actions" and "behavior." Here we seem
to be in the realm of fact. Either a thing acts or
it does not. Here there is no room for interpretation. We are in the area of objectively apprehen-
sible reality. At least our language is. But from
the fact that we talk about "actions" and "be-

havior," does it follow that we know what we are talking about? Just what do we mean by a judge's "actions" as distinguished from his meanings and intentions? Is it a movement of the arms or of the jaws? Is it a movement at all? If not, what is it?

In the spirit of the American realist school, Kornfeld takes a distinction between legal *principles* (which are mere subjective ideals) and legal *rules* (which actually get themselves realized in men's actions). Lundstedt, in commenting on this distinction, points out that Kornfeld nowhere produces an illustration of what he calls a legal *rule*, so that his program for a purely factual and empirical description of legal phenomena is never put to the test of practical application.[16] I may say that although I have read a good many articles expounding the view that the law—that is, the *true* law—consists in the behavior patterns of judges, I have never yet seen one of these patterns, and I cannot claim to have the slightest notion what one of them would look like.

[16] 1 DIE UNWISSENSCHAFTLICHKEIT DER RECHTSWISSENSCHAFT (1932) 325.

LECTURE II

It can be said, I think, that realistic positivism transports to its own more factual field the same error of method which vitiated Austin's theory. The error in both cases consists in assuming that the taking of a distinction implies a kind of permanent bisection of the subject matter involved, and that if I can point to a difference between *Fact A* and *Fact B* it must follow that these two facts fall into sharply divided and mutually exclusive areas of reality. If we start with Austin, it is perfectly clear that there *is* a difference in the effectiveness with which rules impose themselves on men, and that there is also a difference in the degree to which particular rules are backed by an organized machinery of enforcement. Austin concluded from the fact that these differences exist that if one searched hard enough one would be able to find some criterion which would sharply distinguish law from morality, which of course does not follow at all.

Likewise realism starts with an undoubted fact, that it is often possible to formulate rules which more adequately express the motives on which judges act than do the rules "laid down" by

58

the judges themselves.[17] The realists pass over from this undoubted fact to the conclusion that there must exist a sharp line between the rules that judges act on and those they talk about; that there must exist a field which is pure judicial behavior and nothing else. The error is equivalent to supposing that because one can definitely assert that *Point A* is north of *Point B* it must follow that there exists some dividing line beyond which everything is North and below which everything is South. There is no such thing as a field which consists simply of judicial behavior; it is in fact a greater phantom than Austin's sovereign, which at least had the merit of corresponding to something in the ordinary man's thinking about law.

It may seem that in what I have so far said about legal realism I have placed a disproportionate emphasis on the realist definition of law, and that I have sought to dispose of a whole movement by attacking one of its intellectual appendages. My basic criticism of the realist movement is not, however, directed against its definition of law, but

[17] Ihering's discussion of this phenomenon of "latent rules," written in 1852, remains, I believe, unsurpassed. 1 GEIST DES RÖMISCHEN RECHTS (7th ed. 1924) §3.

against the positivistic spirit of which this definition is a symptom. I do not care how realism defines words, but I am concerned with the way it
directs the application of human energies in the
law.[18] If we look at the movement in that light,
I think we can say that its program has been largely
shaped by two, and possibly three, assumptions.
First, the realists have assumed that a rigorous
separation of *is* and *ought* is possible, and that one
may study the law in isolation from its ethical
context.[19] *Secondly,* they have assumed that this
separation of *is* and *ought* is something so obviously
desirable that it is not necessary to justify the

[18] *Cf.,* " . . . I am not going to attempt a definition of law.
. . . I shall instead devote my attention to the *focus* of mat-
ters legal." Llewellyn, *A Realistic Jurisprudence,* 30 COL. L.
REV. 431, 432.

[19] This assumption runs through the whole realist literature.
Llewellyn has remarked that perhaps Pound could be cited
for all planks of the realistic platform with the possible exception of "the rigorous temporary severance of Is and
Ought." *Some Realism about Realism* (1931) 44 HARV. L.
REV. 1222, 1255, n. 114. This observation—which, it should
be said, was made somewhat casually—seems to constitute a
recognition that the most distinctive contribution of the
realist movement has been its insistence on a separation of
the *is* and the *ought.*

expenditure of human energy needed to achieve it. *Thirdly*—and here we must depend to a greater degree on inference—they have apparently assumed that nothing worthwhile can be said about the *ought* until after the *is* has been scientifically and exhaustively charted. These assumptions are, in my opinion, false, and to the extent that they have been taken seriously their effects on American legal thinking have been injurious.

Fortunately, they have not always been taken seriously, even by the leaders of the movement. Professor Llewellyn, in particular, has given repeated demonstration of a lively and uninhibited interest in "the ethical side of the law," and one gains the impression that a "rigorous severance of *is* and *ought*" is, even as a theory, becoming every year less evident in his writings. But we must judge a movement not simply in terms of the practices of its ablest exponents, but also in terms of its effects on the main body of those whose activities it touches. Viewed in this aspect, the realist movement seems to me to have continued, and even to have reinforced, the positivistic bent which has restrained legal thinking in this country now for nearly a century. However seriously the realist definition of law may be taken, it has in military parlance created a diversion behind which the positivistic attitude has been able to gain an extension of life. By giving legal positivism an appearance of modernity and sophistication, the realist movement has made continued adherence to that position intellectually respectable, and has encouraged the natural sloth which clings to positivism as the only way of escaping what the practical lawyer horrendously describes as "philosophy."

Even in the case of its most discerning adherents, it is by no means clear that the realist view has always been lacking in an inhibitive effect. One may cite here the example of the most illustrious realist of them all, Justice Oliver Wendell Holmes. Certainly it cannot be said that the positivism of his early essays was ever completely sloughed off during his career as a judge. One who surveys his contributions to the American common law and compares them with those, let us say, of Cardozo, cannot escape a sense of disappointment. Even his most ardent admirers will have to admit, I believe, that his influence as a judge—at least in the field of private law—fell far short of being commensurate with his general intellectual stature.[20] For him the notion that the law is something severable from one's notions of what it ought to be seems to have had a real and inhibitive meaning. One may admire his fidelity to a faith. But was it for the ultimate good of our law? I think there is reason to doubt it.

My discussion of the realist movement would not be complete if I left the impression that its effects on legal thinking in this country have been wholly negative and restraining. Nothing could be farther from the fact. It should be recalled that I am concerned with the realist movement here only insofar as it affects the subject of these lectures, which is the issue of natural law *versus* legal positivism. The realists have made important contributions to legal thinking which have no direct relevance to that issue. Professor Walter Wheeler Cook's perennial war against the sort of verbal trifling that Mach called "unconscious metaphysics," for example, deserves the support of all schools of legal

20 "No branch of American law can be said to have been molded by him." Cohen, *A Critical Sketch of Legal Philosophy in America*, in 2 LAW—A CENTURY OF PROGRESS (pub. by New York Univ. Press, 1937) 266, 302.

philosophy.[21] In another place[22] I have attempted
to appraise this and such other aspects of the realist
movement as are not directly concerned here. I
should like to add only one further observation,
which is that the realists seem to me to have carried
over into the field of factual inquiry something of
the same error of method that they have applied
to the study of legal phenomena. They have failed
sufficiently to realize that in the moving world of
fact, as in the moving world of law, the *is* and the
ought are inseparably mixed. The result has been

[21] The following words written by John Stuart Mill can, I
believe, be applied to Professor Cook with more justice than
to their original subject: "Mr. Austin once said of himself,
that if he had any special intellectual vocation it was that of
'untying knots.' In this judgment he estimated his own
qualifications very correctly. The untying of intellectual
knots; the clearing up of the puzzles arising from complex
combinations of ideas confusedly apprehended, and not
analysed into their elements; the building up of definite conceptions where only indefinite ones existed, and where the
current phrases disguised and perpetuated the indefinite-
ness . . . these were, of the many admirable characteristics
of Mr. Austin's work as a jurist, those which most especially
distinguished him." Quoted in HOLDSWORTH, SOME MAKERS
OF ENGLISH LAW (1938) 261-262.

[22] *American Legal Realism* (1934) 82 U. OF PA. L. REV. 429;
reprinted in 76 PROC. OF AM. PHIL. SOC. (1936) 191.

a strong preference for those facts which can be statistically or graphically presented; a specious objectivity has been bought at the cost of significant, if intangible, realities. The facts most relevant to legal study will generally be found to be what may be called moral facts. They lie not in behavior patterns, but in attitudes and conceptions of rightness, in the obscure taboos and hidden reciprocities which permeate business and social relations. They are facts of a type which will not pass readily through a Hollerith statistical sorting machine, and they require for their investigation and interpretation not so much the talents of the statistician as those of a good ethnologist who can feel his way into a complex and unfamiliar moral environment. That facts of this sort have been neglected has been due in part, I believe, to an attempt to carry over into the field of fact the same separation of *is* and *ought* that is considered essential in the law.[23]

23 Since these words were written Professor Nussbaum has published a comprehensive critique of the methods of factual research employed in this country and in Germany. *Fact Research in Law* (1940) 40 COL. L. REV. 189. I am happy to see my general conclusions confirmed by his, since he speaks from a background of experience much richer than my own. American legal scholars could profit greatly from

Lecture II

In turning now to the theory of Hans Kelsen,[24]
I think the best approach is to regard it as being
in part a reaction against the realist, or as he calls
it, "sociological" tendency we have just discussed,

---

a study of the common-sense *reportage* of relevant facts of
all kinds exemplified in his Lehrbuch des deutschen
Hypothekenwesens (1921). Free from self-conscious limitations of method, the book neglects neither statistics nor
the homely kind of information one can gain only through
first-hand contact with those experienced in a particular
field. In this country an outstanding contribution toward
making available facts of the "non-statistical" variety has been
that of Professor David F. Cavers through his editorship of
Law and Contemporary Problems. It was in preparing
an article for this journal that a realization was brought
home to me of the tremendous importance of such facts for
the law. See *The Special Nature of the Wage-Earner's Life
Insurance Problem* (1935) 2 Law & Contemp. Prob. 10.

24 A very complete bibliography of writings by and about
the "Vienna School" will be found in the appendix to Kelsen's Reine Rechtslehre (1934). Very little of Kelsen's work
has been translated into English. However, there are available in that language at least two articles by him: *The Pure
Theory of Law* (1934) 50 L. Q. Rev. 474 and (1935) 51 *id.* 203;
and *The Function of the Pure Theory of Law* (New York
Univ. Press, 1937) 2 Law—A Century of Progress 231.

Useful commentaries on the work of the school will be
found in: Lauterpacht, *Kelsen's Pure Theory of Law* in
Modern Theories of Law (1933) 105; Voegelin, *Kelsen's
Pure Theory of Law* (1927) 42 Pol. Sci. Q. 268; Kunz, *The
Vienna School and International Law* (1934) 11 N. Y. U. L. Q.

66

for, as we have noted, there were counterparts of
the American tendency in the Continental literature when Kelsen began his work. Kelsen's ob-
jection to the realist direction of legal positivism
may be briefly stated as follows. Though as positivists we are interested in the law *that is* to the
exclusion of the question what it ought to be, this
existing law is itself a norm or *ought*. A conception of law which is incapable of yielding norms
is of no value to the positivist, and this is the fatal
defect in the realist view. If law is merely the way
people behave, how are we to tell when they are
misbehaving? Suppose we admit that the law consists in sequences or regularities in the actions of
state officials. What imperative or "ought" follows from this? None at all. To be sure, we may
say that if we wish to avoid unpleasant clashes we

REV. 370; EBENSTEIN, DIE RECHTSPHILOSOPHISCHE SCHULE DER
REINEN RECHTSLEHRE (1938).

The principal members of the "Vienna School" beside
Kelsen himself are Adolf Merkl, Alfred Verdross, and
František Weyr. The outstanding apostate is Fritz Sander,
though even he seems to remain obscurely faithful to the
positivistic principle. It is characteristic that in the quarrel
between Sander and Kelsen each accuses the other of the
sin of "natural law."

ought to synchronize our behavior with that of the state officials. But this bit of practical wisdom does not follow from the theory that the law is official behavior, and it would be equally applicable if we were under the domination of a mere robber band which made no pretense of enforcing a legal order. The realist theory, then, having sunk itself in the bed of reality, is incapable of returning to the field of "oughts," and is in fact not properly a legal study at all.[25]

It should be noted that Austin's theory is not subject to this criticism. Austin's theory yielded *oughts*. It kept in mind that the primary purpose of positivism is to distinguish between two kinds of competing *oughts*, those which have been lifted to the rank of law and those which have not. Accordingly, when a given *ought* satisfied Austin's theory, that is, if it was a command of the sovereign, it was quite immaterial what specific people did about it; it remained a rule of law (and carried with it whatever particular "oughtness" followed from that characterization) though it was ignored

[25] EBENSTEIN, DIE RECHTSPHILOSOPHISCHE SCHULE DER REINEN RECHTSLEHRE (1938) 54.

by laymen and judges alike. The unobeyed and ineffective law remained a law.[26] The difficulty with Austin and similar thinkers lay in their attempt to tie their test of legal "oughtness" to some external fact. Their sovereign was set up to establish a boundary about the field of law, and yet the sovereign could itself only be defined in legal terms. The theory of sovereignty seems, then, to involve a begging of the question which positivism sets out to answer.

Kelsen's contribution was in effect to say: Since we must beg the question, let us do so openly and with as little circumlocution as possible. Everyone knows that the sovereign is not a real thing; let us cease pretending that it is. Instead let us look to see what purpose it serves, and adopt the minimum of assumptions necessary to the accomplishment of that purpose. The sovereign makes legal positivism possible by introducing into the legal

---

[26] This assumption is necessarily implied in Austin's definition of law and in his definition of the sovereign. The point is explicitly made in SOMLÓ, JURISTISCHE GRUNDLEHRE §35. Gray regarded a rule "laid down" by the courts as law even though it was not obeyed by the public. THE NATURE AND SOURCES OF THE LAW (2d ed. 1921) 105.

order a principle of unity. Very well, since in the end this indispensable unity is going to result from postulating something, let us postulate it directly, avoiding the intellectual detours involved in metaphors and personificative fictions. All that is necessary is to assume some basic rule or norm which can furnish a kind of constitution for the legal order.[27] Those things will then be law which happen in accordance with, and derive their valid-

[27] In his REINE RECHTSLEHRE (p. 66) Kelsen says that the basic norm is "merely the expression of the hypothesis necessarily assumed in every positivistic treatment of the material of the law." He adds that the basic norm is not "established" or "enacted" but is "presupposed" as a condition of the positivistic legal method. In another place [DIE PHILOSOPHISCHEN GRUNDLAGEN DER NATURRECHTSLEHRE UND DES RECHTSPOSITIVISMUS (1928) p. 12] he asserts that the basic norm is "only the formulation of the necessary premise underlying any positivistic conception of legal phenomena. It only raises to consciousness what all lawyers do, though often unconsciously, when in conceiving of the subject matter of their science they reject natural law (or in other words, restrict themselves to the positive law), and at the same time regard the thing they study, not as a phenomenon of power, but as law, not as a mere fact, but as a norm." He says later in the same work (p. 26) that the conception of the basic norm does not create a new method "but by analysing the procedure actually followed by legal science simply lays bare the logical presuppositions of a method long familiar."

ity from, this assumed basic norm—which of course has neither a beard nor a sceptre.

With the disappearance of the sovereign, the notion of the sovereign's agents also goes by the board. After all, to say that the little law maker acts on behalf of the big law maker involves a needlessly metaphorical way of getting what we are after. All we need to say is that we conceive of the legal order as forming a sort of hierarchy in which those things happening on the lower levels derive their validity from the fact that they happen within the framework established by the higher levels of the order. This hierarchic or pyramidal view is simply a recognition, with a minimum of metaphor, that although our legal order is complex it is viewed as forming a unity, and that it contains within itself the necessary apparatus for resolving conflicts.[28] Under this view, when the judge makes law he is not making it on behalf of anyone else; he is simply exercising a function allotted to him under an assumed constitutional order.

[28] This theory of the *Stufenbau* of the law was first developed by Merkl, though it has been adopted by Kelsen. See KELSEN, HAUPTPROBLEME DER STAATSRECHTSLEHRE (2d ed. 1923) xv.

Lecture II

It has been said of Kelsen that his principal service has been to reduce legal positivism to an absurdity.[29] I think it would be truer and fairer to say that he has made an honest fiction out of positivism. This is no inconsiderable service. As long as the impulse toward positivism, the desire for some criterion of the law *that is,* found its expression in such imaginative creatures as the Sovereign and his Agents, clear thinking in the law was im-

[29] "Ohne jede Ironie sehe ich . . . Kelsens grösstes Verdienst darin, den logistischen Rechtspositivismus in der Staatslehre dadurch, dass er ihn ohne Konzessionen mit dem grössten Nachdruck und überragendem Scharfsinn vertreten hat, endgültig ad absurdam geführt zu haben." Heller, *Die Krisis der Staatslehre* (1926) 55 ARCHIV FÜR SOZIALWISSEN-SCHAFT UND SOZIALPOLITIK 289, 309.

In this article—which one cannot read today without some sense of the doom which then hung over the German social structure—Heller comments on the extent to which in Germany public law and political science had become passively positivistic. He remarks that the foreign writings most esteemed abroad were unacceptable in Germany because, being tainted by ethics and natural law, they were not deemed sufficiently "scientific." In an article on German legal science written about the same time, Voegelin observed with apparent satisfaction that in Germany "to be found guilty of adherence to natural law theories is a kind of social disgrace." *Kelsen's Pure Theory of Law* (1927) 42 POL. SCI. QUAR. 268, 269.

possible. The whole field was cluttered up with metaphysical entities, which not only suggested false analogies, but were obstacles to the drawing of more fruitful ones. It is largely because of his service in ridding positivism of its superfluous baggage that Kelsen can be referred to as one of the most influential jurists alive today.[30]

It is true that in later years Kelsen's theory has been given a less negative aspect, chiefly by his followers, though to some extent by himself. This is accomplished through the importation of certain Kantian notions which Kant did not himself apply to the law, and which did not in fact influence, at least directly or substantially, the original formulation of Kelsen's theory.[31] It is now said, in effect,

[30] Articles and books by Kelsen have been translated into the following languages: Czech, English, French, Greek, Hungarian, Italian, Japanese, Polish, Rumanian, Serbian, and Spanish. See the *Appendix* to his REINE RECHTSLEHRE (1934). He is also well known in Holland and Scandinavia, where, of course, translations are not needed. The *Appendix* cited above includes a bibliography of books and articles having to do with the "pure theory of law." The list runs to about nine hundred items.

[31] See Kelsen's own statement in the introduction to his HAUPTPROBLEME DER STAATSRECHTSLEHRE (2d ed. 1923) xvii.

that Kelsen's theory concerns itself with certain
categories of legal thought. Just as in Kant's view
our experience of the outer world in coming to
us passes through, and is transformed by, certain
categories of thought, such as cause and effect, so,
according to this view of the Vienna School, the
raw material of the law is only apperceptible by us
in terms of certain unifying ideas. Of course, by
bringing in these Kantian ideas, the Vienna School
has opened the field for a repetition of all the disputes which have raged about the interpretation
of Kant's *Critique.* Are these "forms of legal
thought" wholly subjective? If not, just how
"subjective" are they? Are they only forms that
people have got in the habit of using in thinking
about law, or are they what Austin called "necessary legal notions" without which legal thinking
is impossible? Are they static and given for all
time, or are they subject to evolution? I shall not
go into these questions except to say that I do not
for a moment believe that Kelsen is analysing "the

"It is historically true . . . that Kelsen's first principal work
. . . was an intuitive creation, written with no profound
knowledge of Kant . . . " Kunz, *The "Vienna School" and
International Law* (1924) 11 N.Y.U.L.Q. 370, 372, n. 9.

necessary forms of legal thought." What he is analysing are simply the assumptions which customarily underlie positivistic thinking about law, these assumptions being in turn the expression, conscious or unconscious, of certain ethical desiderata which were discussed openly by Hobbes, but which have been passed over in silence by most positivists since his time.[32]

[32] An exception is perhaps Dickinson. The following excerpts from his article, *A Working Theory of Sovereignty* (1927) 42 POL. SCI. Q. 524, (1928) 43 *id.* 253, indicate sufficiently the quality of his legal positivism. After each passage I have inserted in brackets the name of the author whose views are suggested. "Men obviously need no sovereign to exercise a prerogative of choice in order to tell them whether twice two is five or four. If the laws which distinguish right from wrong are equally well defined by 'nature', we need no sovereign to tell us whether the issue of watered stock by a corporation is illegal, or whether or not relief by injunction is a lawful remedy to apply in a labor dispute." [Hobbes] "The importance of thus ear-marking the ultimate lawgiving organ by attaching to it the word 'sovereign' springs from the importance of keeping the idea of 'law' distinct from the other kinds of rules and imperatives which have an influence upon human conduct and relations." [Austin] "*Sovereignty in the legal sense* is after all nothing more nor less than a logical postulate or presupposition of any system of order according to law." [Kelsen] Dickinson's article leaves unanswered the important question whether the ethical need for peace and order can be satisfied by a

75

LECTURE II

It is often observed that extreme points of view have a kind of hidden affinity, as if in traveling away from the middle ground each had completed the same circuit from opposite directions. This reconciliation of seeming opposites is, I think, present to some degree in the realist and Kelsenian views, for these two schools of thought have much in common both in their methods and in the results they achieve. Both reject the methodological impurity of the school of the analytical jurists, which pretended to straddle the gap between the world of fact and the world of law with a gaseous sort of monster which purported to be of both worlds. Each sees, what Austin failed to see, that so soon as positivism ceases to serve an ethical purpose and becomes descriptive and "scientific" its road forks sharply, the one branch leading into the realm of pure fact, the other into the realm of pure assumption. Though they take different branches of the fork, each is determined to follow the positivistic approach logically and uncompromisingly in its chosen direction. Each reaps in the end the kind

---

"logical postulate"—whether, in other words, Hobbes' objectives can be attained through an "as-if-istic" sovereign.

76

of reward which usually attends faithful adherence to a consciously imposed limitation of method. The one terminates with a brute observation, the other with a brute assumption; the one ends with things that are true but not significant, the other with things that are significant but not true; the one finds itself left with the stripped seed of positivism, the other with the empty shell.

I have already referred to the similarity between certain aspects of the positivistic viewpoint as worked out by the analytical jurists and some of the doctrines and disputes of theology.[33] I should

---

[33] Kelsen himself has developed in a penetrating way certain analogies between legal and theological thinking. See especially his DER SOZIOLOGISCHE UND DER JURISTISCHE STAATS-BEGRIFF (2d ed. 1928) §§36-45, and ALLGEMEINE STAATSLEHRE (1925) §16. In the first work cited he recognizes that his view resembles pantheism in rejecting the dualism of state and law. In another place he likens legal positivism to the notion of a revealed religion. DIE PHILOSOPHISCHEN GRUND-LAGEN DER NATURRECHTSLEHRE UND DES RECHTSPOSITIVIS-MUS (1928) p. 67. If this second analogy is intended to be applied to his own theory it is far from apt. The difficulty of making any practical application of "the pure theory of law" lies precisely in the fact that it possesses no authoritative revelation of the law. It only asserts that the law ought to derive its validity from some single source, and that men assume the existence of some

like to develop this similarity at greater length, covering the whole history of the positivistic philosophy. Like all analogies this one cannot be pressed too far, and I should certainly not want to make the stream of legal philosophy even more turgid by releasing into it the emotions which have sometimes colored the most abstract points of theology. Nor do I pretend that the appraisals reached in the one field can be transferred directly to the other, for there is in religion a legitimate element of mysticism which is not present or ought not to be present in jurisprudence.

Taking legal philosophy as it existed prior to the development of the notion of sovereignty by

------

such source in their thinking and talking about the law. It never defines that source in terms which are objectively descriptive. The inappositeness of the analogy to revealed religion becomes doubly manifest when it is recalled that the Vienna School insists that its theory is "dynamic" and embraces a positive law with a changing content. Even its hypothetical and undefined Bible is, then, a Bible which changes daily, and of course the elimination of "anthropomorphic" elements in jurisprudence has left us without a Moses who might serve as the author of these changes. Certainly this Moses is not to be found in the Vienna School itself, for by their own profession their theory does not *create* rules of law but only *recognizes* them.

Hobbes, Bodin, and others, we may say that it re-
sembled polytheism. The whole field of law and
morality—no hard and fast line being drawn between the two—was presided over by a number of
deities. We can distinguish at least four: Reason,
Custom, Agreement, and Coercive Power. All of
these were considered capable of ordering the relations of men. As in the case of the ancient
heathen gods, no very neat division of labor had
been worked out among them. Sometimes they
worked together; sometimes they were in conflict.
Each had a sort of natural field, but was never
secure from the encroachments of the others. In
cases of conflict, no superior power existed which
was capable of reconciling their differences. Men
were apparently no more disturbed by this than
they were by the Olympian struggles of their gods,
in which they took a kind of zestful bystander's
interest. The question who was supreme bothered
only the philosophers, and in general—no doubt
through a kind of professional bias—they inclined
in favor of Reason.

With Hobbes we have reached the stage of complete monotheism. In place of the capricious and
quarreling deities which previously divided the

LECTURE II

field among themselves, we now have one supreme
power ruling over the whole legal universe. As in
the case of monotheism, our old deities are not so
much banished from the field, as absorbed in a
larger unity. Custom, for example, still makes law,
but only when and to the extent that it is permitted
to do so by the sovereign power.

Hobbes wrote that it stood "with the mysteries
of our Religion as with wholesome pills for the
sick, which swallowed whole, have the vertue to
cure; but chewed, are for the most part cast up
again without effect."[34] Reading between the lines,
the analytical jurists might well have understood
this admonition to apply not only to religion but
to Hobbes' theory of sovereignty as well. For most
of their difficulties arose from their having begun
to chew over the doctrine of sovereignty.

Taken on faith, that is, as setting up an ethical
goal to be attained with as little compromise as
possible, Hobbes' view is perhaps capable of as
much good in the political and legal field as a
simple and unintellectualized faith in the deity is
in a man's inner life. But there are jurists, as well

[34] LEVIATHAN 287 [195].

80

as theologians, who are too cerebral to leave the matter there. There is, indeed, a close parallel between theoretical theology and analytical jurisprudence; the questions which have agitated both show a surprising correspondence, as if the human mind were repeating in the one field the same gropings and gyrations that it had already followed in the other. In theology we have the question, "If God is the cause of all things, who then caused God?" In legal theory we have the question, "If the Sovereign defines what is law, how, then, can there be a legal definition of the Sovereign?" In both fields men have racked their brains over such questions as whether unlimited power carries with it the capacity to impose limitations on itself. To deny to omnipotence such a capacity seems to deprive it of one kind of power, and yet the exercise of such a power would destroy the very omnipotence postulated. Other parallels, not so immediately apparent, can be drawn. There is, for example, a basic similarity between the doctrine of infant damnation and the notion of a gapless law. Both assume the existence of a closed system of norms, and deny the possibility of the unprovided-for case.

The view that I have called "realism" finds its

LECTURE II

rather obvious counterpart in pantheism. These two
views resemble each other not only in their historical origins, but also in the fact that neither can be
understood without reference to those origins. The
assertion that God is everything, or that everything
in the universe is God, would be perfect nonsense
to one who was not familiar with the views which
preceded it and the difficulties it was intended to
resolve. So also, I think, the realist conception of
law can only be understood against the background
of the theory of sovereignty it supplanted.

Legal realism and pantheism are attempted solutions of the same fundamental difficulty. Legal
positivism begins by seeking some unifying force
which will give coherence to the legal system and
offer a clear-cut definition of law. It finds this
unifying force in a sovereign power. On reflection,
however, it discovers that this sovereign power
cannot, in most modern states, be a single person.
Today we can no longer believe in a personal
sovereign. On the other hand, if the sovereign is
not a person, then it is a mere abstraction, and to
make a distinction between the governmental system itself and this sovereign power which inheres
in it and runs it, seems to involve a duplication of

82

what is in fact but a single thing. Hence we end by asserting that the sovereign is merely the governmental system, and the law is the way that system functions. Meanwhile, however, it may escape our notice that in completing the circuit, we have lost the thing we started out to find, which was some test which would enable us to say when a rule should be given that particular sanction due rules of law. Our quest for a unifying principle has doubled back on itself, and, ending where it started, has given us a barren tautology instead of a solution for our problem.

The theory of the Vienna School is like that of those cautious and sophisticated modern religions which say, in effect, "We do not know whether there is a God, but if there is, then if He is to fulfil His divine purpose His attributes will have to be as follows." Though the Vienna School claims in general to keep its theory "pure" of the contamination of ethical considerations, there are occasionally hints of an attitude somewhat similar to that William James expressed when he said, or almost said, that by believing in God we may help Him to exist.

In theology, as in jurisprudence, opposites sometimes meet. I have already spoken of a kind of covert affinity existing between legal realism and the Vienna School. So, too, though pantheism and religious "as-if-ism'' seem in one aspect diametrically opposed, it is obvious that to say that the universe is God comes very close to saying that God is only a way of looking at the universe.

Leaving the theological analogy, I should like to return to a fundamental question which I raised at the very outset of our historical survey of legal positivism. Just what are the positivists trying to do? We know, of course, that they seek some means of drawing a sharp line between law and morality, between the law *that is,* on the one hand, the law that ought to be, or is trying to be, on the other. We know also that the positivists since Hobbes have almost without exception denied that they were drawing this line for ethical or political reasons.[35]

[35] Of course even the most rigorously "scientific" positivist will not be able to resist altogether the temptation to claim, as a kind of by-merit of his theory, that its practical effects are more desirable than those of natural law. Austin himself devotes a short paragraph to an observation that the sovereign power is made "necessary or highly expedient" by "the uncertainty, scantiness, and imperfection of positive moral rules." JURISPRUDENCE p. 302, n. 28. More surprisingly, the author of "the pure theory of law" has in one

They insist that their primary object is to promote clear thinking in the law. There can be no doubt that individual positivists, like Kelsen, have done much to purge positivism's own procedures of obscurity. They have advanced the law's quest of itself by rescuing it from unprofitable by-paths and detours. But the question remains whether the end sought in this quest is itself worth the candle. Would clarity in legal discussion actually be advanced if positivism could attain its objective of some clear-cut distinction between law and morality?

———

passage made what appears to be a kind of off-the-record admission that the preference for positivism over natural law may rest ultimately on an emotional bias in favor of the ideal of peace as against that of justice. Kelsen, DIE IDEE DES NATURRECHTS (1927) 7 ZEITSCHRIFT FÜR ÖFFENTLICHES RECHT 221, 248. In a somewhat similar mood of concession, Kelsen admits in another place [DIE PHILOSOPHISCHEN GRUND-LAGEN DER NATURRECHTSLEHRE UND DES RECHTSPOSITIVIS-MUS (1928) 66] that the notion of the "basic norm" involves a departure from strict positivism. He insists, however, that the natural-law element in the basic norm is reduced to the minimum necessary to support any system of positive law. This recalls Pascal's remark about Descartes, that he would have preferred to get along without God, but needed Him to start his universe going—after which he had no further use for Him. PENSÉES §77.

The drawing of distinctions is certainly not an activity which can be justified as an end in itself. If I were to write a long treatise devoted to developing and maintaining a sharp distinction between the concepts "pie" and "cake," disposing definitively of all the hard borderline cases, like Boston cream pie and upside-down cake, I could scarcely look forward to being congratulated on my contribution to the clarification of a difficult subject. Nor will it do to say that the efforts made to distinguish law and morality are justified by the importance of the subject matter involved, any more than I could support my exercise in culinary taxonomy by pointing out that it dealt with the important subject of human nutriment. The question is not whether law and morality are important. The question is whether drawing a sharp line between the two is important. Hobbes thought so, and unlike his successors, he gave a definite reason why he thought so. He wanted men to obey even those rules of law which they were convinced were unjust. He had no desire to extend this appeal to the whole field of morality. His "law," then, was a particular segment cut out of the larger field of morality for the purpose of receiving a special sanction, which in turn found its justification in the primary need for peace and order. His distinction was framed with reference to a definite political goal; his positivism was firmly anchored in natural law.

The later positivists are, by their own profession, not politicians but logicians and analysts. They assert that their distinctions are justified by the fact that people who do not observe them confuse law and morality and are in consequence unable to think clearly. This means one of two things: either that other people when they "confuse" law and morality do not take a distinction which the positivists do—in which case the question of the justification for the distinction is begged; or it means that other people take a distinction between law and morality, but take it confusedly and badly, in which case positivism becomes merely an exercise in clarifying linguistic usage, distinguished from other such studies by the fact that it makes the claim to be able to analyse a distinction without reference to the purposes it serves. There is, in fact, much implicit recognition in the literature of positivism that it is primarily an analysis of the usages of legal language. Maine comments on the frequency of Austin's appeal to the sense of absurdity, as where he refuses to apply his theory of sovereignty to the primitive family, not because it will not fit, but because such an application would seem "absurd," that is, would violate the normal usages of language.[86] In expounding their own particular brands of positivism, both Timasheff and Somló reject certain conceptions of law as not being in accord with the "facts."[87] What facts are involved is not stated; they are apparently facts of linguistic usage. That the Vienna School purports to be analysing the necessary forms of legal thought need not conceal the fact that it may merely be analysing the customary forms of legal language.[88]

The purely formal and verbal nature of the conclusions of legal positivism is revealed in the inability of positivism, in all its forms, to deal with the *content* of the law. Not only has positivism failed in its quest for some definite criterion of the law *that is,* but it has failed to say anything signifi-

[86] Maine, The Early History of Institutions (1874) 379.

[87] Timasheff, An Introduction to the Sociology of Law (1939) 142, 166, 277; Somló, Juristische Grundlehre (2d ed. 1927) 205, 300.

[88] *Cf.* the translated passages from Kelsen in note 27 *supra.*

cant concerning the law which it assumes to "be."
Even within the framework of its own premises it
remains formal and sterile. Such pressing problems
as the proper attitude of the judge toward statutes
and previous decisions are left without answer.
Kelsen in particular is impatient with any discussion of theories of interpretation.[39] These things
belong to politics, not to law. How the judge
arrives at his decision is a "meta-legal" question
without interest for the jurist. Kelsen limits his insistence to asserting that after the decision has been
rendered it must be viewed as deriving its validity
from an assumed basic norm. The realist insists
that it be viewed as a pattern of official behavior.
Is the difference between these two views worth
quarreling over, since neither has any possible
relevance to the decisions you and I as citizens may
be called upon to make?

It is in this matter of dealing with the content
of the law that the uncomfortable dilemma of
modern positivism becomes most apparent. Natu-

[39] See REINE RECHTSLEHRE (1934) p. 94 *et seq*. Austin's treatment of the problem of interpretation would be regarded
from the standpoint of the Vienna School as a departure
from "pure" positivism. JURISPRUDENCE 1023-1036.

rally any legal theorist would like his theories to
serve some useful purpose, and this means that they
ought to have something significant to say about
the actual content of the law. On the other hand,
positivism cannot permit its desire to be useful to
interfere with its chance of achieving some formal
criterion which will separate law from morality, for
if that criterion is lost, of course positivism is lost
with it. Unfortunately, however, positivism finds
itself in a situation where it seems impossible for
it to be useful and positivistic at the same time.

Positivism could, of course, be useful if it pro-
moted peace and order. If this is its object, clearly
it must concern itself with the content of the law,
and not only with the content but with the "goodness" of that content. The stability of a given legal
system, its capacity to produce peace and order,
will depend not simply on the lawyer's faithful
adherence to its enacted rules,[40] but also on the lay-

---

[40] Of course, even from the standpoint of the lawyer legal
certainty is inevitably tied up with the content of legal
rules, as I have tried to show in my article, *American Legal
Realism* (1934) 82 U. OF PA. L. REV. 429, 431-438. This is a
point to which Austin was completely blind. See, for example, his comparison of the binding force of precedents

man's willingness to accept those rules as being essentially right. A law which is "good" for the purpose of establishing order will have to be, or at least to seem, "good" in other respects as well. Yet if positivism begins to view rules in the light of their goodness, it soon finds itself submerged in a fluid and moving reality in which it is impossible to preserve a distinction between what is and what ought to be, or between what has become and what is still trying to be. In attempting to be useful, positivism loses its own positivistic integrity.

The modern solution for this difficulty, as exemplified by the Vienna School, is for positivism to give up trying to be useful. It now presents itself as utterly indifferent to ethics. It has become pure science. It has in fact so purified itself that it has lost its capacity to say anything at all about specific rules of law, or about specific problems of legislation or decision, and confines itself to the terminological insistences I have already mentioned.

In asserting that an attitude toward law cannot

---

in law and in equity. JURISPRUDENCE, 640. He failed to see that it depends upon the content of legal rules and the subject matter with which they deal how far a judge *can* significantly be bound by precedent.

be wholly positivistic and useful at the same time, it may be objected that I have overlooked the art of predicting judicial behavior as it is practiced by the skillful counsellor-at-law. Here is a working attitude toward law which is certainly useful in the sense that it is capable of producing a financial return for its successful practitioner. At the same time it seems positivistic, for certainly the attorney charting a course for his client through legal barriers is not generally preoccupied with natural law or considerations of what ought to be.

But is it so clear that the practitioner is unconcerned with natural law? We may best test the question, I think, by borrowing Holmes' figure of the bad man.[41] For the purpose of drawing a line between law and morality, Holmes suggested that we place ourselves in the position of the bad man, who cares nothing for good and evil or for the praise or blame of his fellows, and who is deterred only by the threat of tangible penalties. By viewing the law through his eyes, we may see it as it really is, washed with cynical acid, and divorced from

[41] *The Path of the Law* (1897), in COLLECTED LEGAL PAPERS (1920) 167.

ethical values. It is a very convincing figure which
he offers us, and it makes a working kind of positivism seem quite plausible. Yet it is apparent that
this bad man of Holmes' is himself an abstraction,
in two senses.

In the first place, it will be noted that it is a
peculiar sort of bad man who is worried about
judicial decrees and is indifferent to extra-legal
penalties, who is concerned about a fine of two
dollars but apparently not about the possible loss
of friends and customers. To define the law in
terms of the viewpoint of one with this attitude is
to some extent a begging of the question, and
amounts almost to saying that the law is that which
concerns one who is concerned only with the law.

In the second place, Holmes assumes that his
bad man has already reached a conclusion concerning the legal risks of a particular line of conduct,
and he neglects to inquire into the process by which
this man would actually arrive at such a conclusion.
Let us see for ourselves how this bad man, faced
with a specific problem of conduct, would have to
reason. He wants to know what it is likely to cost
him to attain a particular objective. Because of the
peculiarly juristic orientation of his fears, he will

be deterred only by judicial penalties. He must ask himself, then, "What are the chances that my conduct may lead to a detrimental interference in my affairs by the courts?" To answer that, he must ask, "How will my conduct be viewed by judges?" This question he cannot answer merely by consulting the letter of the law, for he will still not know in what direction the letter will be strained in cases of doubt. Nor will it be enough for him "to know his judge." Even if the judge who will decide his case has pronounced and recognizable biases, a bias is, after all, only one factor in a complex equation, and to calculate its effects one must analyse the ethical forces with which it will come in conflict. In the end, our bad man cannot escape having to decide a question of morality. He will have to ask, "How would I myself view my conduct if I were not interested in it? How would it be viewed by a disinterested third party? Would it seem to him to be good or evil?" Only when he has answered this question will he have rounded out the equation on the basis of which he can calculate accurately the chances of judicial intervention in his affairs.

In short, our bad man, if he is effectively to look

after his own interests, will have to learn to look at the law through the eyes of a good man. To be a good positivist, he will have to become a natural-law lawyer.

.

Lecture III

•

Systems of Natural Law and the
Natural-Law Method

•

The Emotional Foundations of Positivism

•

The Possibility of an Autonomous Order

•

Positivistic Influences
in Modern Legal Thinking

III

SO FAR we have been almost exclusively concerned with the difficulties encountered in the search for some criterion which will separate the law that is from the law that ought to be. Our attention has been concentrated on the obstacles which beset the law's quest of itself. I have attempted to reveal the essentially sterile nature of any form of legal positivism which purports to divorce itself from a definite ethical or practical goal; I have tried to demonstrate the bankruptcy of those formalized varieties of positivism which purport to deal analytically and descriptively with an assumed "pure fact of law." Does this rejection of the claims of "scientific" positivism imply a recommendation that we should go the whole way in the opposite direction of legal thought? Am I to be understood as asserting, in effect, that almost any system of natural law is to be preferred to legal positivism? If not, then what attitude is here implied toward the various theories of natural

99

law that have come down to us from the speculations of the past?

In answering these questions, I should like to
have it understood at the outset that any compli-
ments which may here be cast in the direction of
natural law are not addressed to the doctrine of
natural and inalienable rights. This warning
would probably be unnecessary if it were not for
the fact that we have got into the habit of identi-
fying these two notions and of assuming that some
conception of the natural rights of man must lie
at the heart of every system of natural law. As
a matter of fact, if we take into account the whole
course of legal philosophy from its beginnings with
the Greeks, the notion of natural rights appears
not as an integral part of the theory of natural
law but as a passing episode in the history of
ethical and legal speculation. Even in its heyday
the view was neither received unanimously, nor
entertained by its philosophic adherents in the
unqualified form it assumed in political docu-
ments. But there is no need here either to beat
dead horses or to review their pedigrees. I am
not advocating the doctrine of natural rights, and
I may add that in my opinion the notion of "im-

puted rights," or rights in the positivistic sense, is open to many of the objections which have been advanced against natural rights.

Not only am I not proposing to re-fight the philosophic battles of the American and French Revolutions, but I am not attempting to set myself up as sponsor for any of the various systems of natural law which have been advocated in the past. In particular, I should dislike being called upon to undertake a defense of all the things which have been said in the name of that excellent philosopher, Saint Thomas Aquinas. On the other hand, I believe that there is much of great value for the present day in the writings of those thinkers who are classified, and generally dismissed, as belonging to the school of natural law, and I regard it as one of the most unfortunate effects of the positivistic trend still current that it has contributed to bring about the neglect of this important and fruitful body of literature. Ironically enough, one of the things which has rendered this literature unacceptable to the modern legal mind is a quality which ought really to have had precisely the opposite effect. It is one of the tenets of modern legal science that law is an integral part of the whole civilization of a society, and that fruitful work in the law presupposes a familiarity with the other social sciences, such as psychology, economics, and sociology. Yet this is only the rediscovery of a point of view which has always been taken for granted in natural-law speculation. Unfortunately for the natural-law philosopher, however, this interest in subjects outside his immediate field has as its price the possibility that his work may soon become dated. By relating his legal philosophy to the other social sciences, he runs the risk that the progress of those sciences may leave his work behind. So today, when we read in Ahrens' *Cours de Droit Naturel* that the theory of evolution is disproved by the fact that monkeys cannot be taught to talk,[1] we put the book back on the shelf in disgust and we forget, or fail to learn, that it contains an excellent discussion of the function of contract law, a discussion which is perhaps even more valuable today than when it was written. We fail also to realize that it was after all more significant that Ahrens' conception of law should

[1] Vol. 1 (8th ed. 1892) p. 254. The discussion of contract law is found in Vol. 1, p. 143, and Vol. 2, p. 223.

have been broad enough to make the truths of biology legally relevant, than that he should have rejected a particular biological theory which was still a great novelty in his day. Of course the work of the positivists is essentially timeless; by abstracting law entirely from its environment and defining it not in terms of its content, but of its form and sanction, they run no risk either of being outdated or of ever contributing anything to the development of the law except restraints and inhibitions. Austin's theory, which suffered no contamination from the backward state of the social sciences of his day, remains today just as true, and just as lacking in significance for human affairs, as in 1832.

The chief value of the older books on natural law for us of the present day does not lie so much in the systems they expound, as in the kind of legal thinking they exemplify. The broader and freer legal method of these books is in a double sense "natural law." In the first place, it is the method men naturally follow when they are not consciously or unconsciously inhibited by a positivistic philosophy. When there is no warning stop sign, reason naturally pushes as far ahead as it can. In the second place, when reason is unhampered by positivistic restraints, it tends inevitably to find anchorage in the natural laws which are assumed to underlie the relations of men and to determine the growth and decay of civilizations.

As I have previously intimated, the restraints which positivism at present imposes on legal thinking, and which prevent us from following this natural method, take the form not so much of specific beliefs as of emotional attitudes. Today it is still positivism which is the sophisticated view. It alone has "brave true things to say." It alone has purified its truths by a thorough washing in cynical acid. Natural law, on the other hand, is a cobwebby illusion, which is either used as a screen for the advancement of selfish interests, or is resorted to in Freudian surrender by souls maladjusted to their environment and unable to look reality in the eye. It is these emotional colorations which are dangerous, not the very slender and generally innocuous intellectual beliefs on which they rest.

If, according to the emotional climate in which we live, romanticism is an unworthy thing, we need to recall that it is not only natural law which makes a romantic and emotional appeal. Positivism has its own bitter-sweet kind of romanticism, all the more attractive because it does not present itself blatantly. Its primary appeal is to the sentiment of loyalty. Sometimes this appeal is put quite soberly and with a minimum of color, as when Hobbes likened government to a game of whist in which the morality consists "in not renouncing trumps."[2] This was a quite legitimate attempt to rally to the support of positivism the sporting instinct which takes pride in knowing and observing the rules of the game. But the glow of virtuous satisfaction which results from having faithfully followed suit is, after all, a limited one, and positivism in search of more colorful analogies passes naturally from the gaming table to the battle field. Perhaps the most eloquent expression of the

[2] "In the same manner as men in playing turn up trump, and as in playing their game their morality consisteth in not renouncing, so in our civil conversation our morality is all contained in not disobeying of the laws." 5 WORKS (ed. Molesworth, 1841) 194. He repeats this figure in another place, where he adds the qualification: ". . . save that in matter of government when nothing else is turned up, clubs are trumps." 6 WORKS 122. In LEVIATHAN (p. 76) he speaks of evil and ambitious men who "hope to mend an ill game . . . by causing a new shuffle."

positivistic faith is that to be found in Tennyson's *Charge of the Light Brigade*. The story of these young men who followed a mistaken command to their deaths because it was not for them to reason why is indeed reminiscent of the emotional attitudes which surround and render spiritually satisfying the positivistic attitude in law. I do not condemn positivism because it appeals to these emotions. I should certainly agree with the creator of Mr. Chips when he says that it is more noble to charge splendidly to one's death because "someone has blundered," than to be driven into battle to the blare of loudspeakers shouting that the leader is always right.[3] But if the appeal is to commendable emotions, it is in the end to emotions and not to reason.

For confirmation of the view that there is often something military about the sentiments which support legal positivism, we need not resort to the familiar remark that Austin learned his jurisprudence in the army. We have only to page through the collected essays of the greatest among

[3] Hilton, *What Mr. Chips Taught Me* (1938) 162 ATLANTIC MONTHLY 28, 39.

American positivists, Justice Oliver Wendell
Holmes. Here military figures greet the eye at
every turn, and it is the picture of the faithful
soldier which illumines the whole edifice of his
philosophy.

Holmes' case suggests furthermore that the positivistic attitude may often represent the emotional
resolution of a conflict between the opposing
forces of romanticism and skepticism at war in
the same breast. Romanticism demands a "fighting faith," the possibility of which skepticism denies.
From the emotional impasse which thus results a
positivistic philosophy may furnish the only possible escape. It offers the faith which romanticism
demands and to which it may make conspicuous
sacrifice. Since this faith is avowedly artificial,
adherence to it involves no compromise of skeptical
scruple.

The psychological theories now popular are more
likely to construe a man's sustaining faiths, not as
the resolution of an inner conflict, but as a screen
to hide his inability to adjust himself to a harsh
outer reality. A favorite device of polemic discussion is to brand the opponent's view as a "de-

fense mechanism." In terms of this psychology it
is, of course, easy to condemn natural law as a
flight from reality. Cohen remarks that the "distinction between what is in fact law and what on
ethical grounds we think ought to be the law is
not a pleasant one to face."[4] No doubt the human
psyche sometimes accommodates itself to this unpleasant fact by denying its existence, and by asserting that the law it thinks ought to be has already
become the law that is. But we must remember
that there are other unpleasant facts in our legal
firmament. One of these is that it is impossible
to take a sharp distinction between the law that is
and the law that ought to be. If the natural-law
philosopher seems to be running in one direction
from reality, we must not overlook the possibility
that the positivist may be traveling at equal speed
in the opposite direction.

What I have just been saying may seem to imply
that positivism and natural law are both founded
on illusions, and are for that reason equally unacceptable. Of course, I do not mean that. In

[4] *A Critical Sketch of Legal Philosophy in America* (1937),
printed in 2 LAW—A CENTURY OF PROGRESS (pub. by New
York Univ. Press, 1937) 266, 285.

the first place, neither view need be founded on an illusion. There were, for example, no visionary excesses about Hobbes' positivism. It rested on a simple recognition of the incapacity of reason to achieve a complete ordering of human relations, and on the need for some arbitrary rule for the sake of peace. Nor does the natural-law turn of thought need to assert more than that it intends to push reason as far as it can. Of course, as Holmes observed, "there is in all men a demand for the superlative." We have a natural hankering for the absolute. We like to think of ourselves, not as pursuing objectives—for there our failure will be too apparent—but as obeying principles, where we can pretend to perfection. The natural-law lawyer does not tell us he is seeking to reduce as much of the law as possible to reason; he customarily asserts that he has discovered the basic principle of justice. The positivist does not tell us he is seeking to promote the ethical desideratum of peace and order, but claims to have discovered the basic fact of law beyond which all research is useless. But if we are to have illusions, let us choose among them intelligently and select that faith which promises the most sustenance for our spiritual needs. The illusion characteristic of natural law is the belief that there is no limit to what human reason can accomplish in regulating the relations of men in society. The illusion characteristic of positivism is the belief that reason can deliberately set itself a limit and stop at this limit. Neither of these designs can be accomplished. We know in advance that we cannot reach our goal of a social order founded solely on reason. But we know equally well that it is impossible to set in advance a stopping place short of our goal beyond which all effort will be in vain. The illusion of natural law has at least this presumption in its favor, that it liberates the energies of men's minds and allows them to accomplish as much as they can.

The most dangerous quality of legal positivism does not lie in its somewhat extravagant affirmations, but in the inhibitive effect it inevitably has upon the development of a spontaneous ordering of human relations, in its denial of the force which ideas have without reference to their human sponsorship. Kelsen asserts that it is characteristic of all forms of natural law that they are *anarchistic* in tendency; they assume the possibility of an ordering of society which rests upon a voluntary acceptance of guiding notions and is not dependent upon any governmental structure.[5] He seems to assume, though apparently he hesitates at open assertion, that no such ordering is possible. As a matter of fact it is clear that it is not only possible, but exists. The bulk of human relations find their regulation outside the field of positive law, however that field may be defined. The existing body of positive law in general serves only to fill that comparatively narrow area of possible dispute where conflicts are not automatically resolved by a reference to tacitly accepted conceptions of rightness. We have cases telling us how mentally deranged a man has to be before he loses the power to make a valid will; we have statutes saying how many witnesses furnish a sufficient guaranty of the authenticity of a will. We need positive law in these cases because without it men might reasonably differ. On the other hand, we do not have cases or statutes telling us whether a will is rendered

[5] DIE PHILOSOPHISCHEN GRUNDLAGEN DER NATURRECHTSLEHRE UND DES RECHTSPOSITIVISMUS (1928) 10; *Naturrecht und positives Recht* (1927) 2 REVUE INTERNATIONALE DE LA THÉORIE DU DROIT 71, 79.

invalid by the fact that the testator wore a green hat while signing it, or whether a newly marketed fountain pen, not in existence when the statutes were passed, is an effective instrument for the expression of testamentary intention. These problems find their regulation outside the positive law, a regulation so automatic that they do not appear as problems at all. In this field of autonomous order which surrounds the positive law there can be no sharp division between the rule that is and the rule that ought to be. The field, being unorganized and formless, permits of no such division. Though there are here neither sovereigns, nor sequences of judicial conduct, nor basic constitutional norms, the chaos of opinion which Hobbes so feared does not exist. Here it is a combination of custom and natural law which rules, and that very effectively.[6]

[6] Of course it is true that this body of non-governmental norms is significantly influenced by "the positive law." See *infra* page 135. This influence of the law over morality exists, however, only because of a kind of tacit presumption that what is "law" is also, in some sense or other, "right." The attitudes which the law thus indirectly shapes derive their sanction, not from their legal origin, but from a public conviction of their "rightness."

Not only does this area of autonomous order exist, but it is changing and growing. Men's judgments of what is fair and right undergo profound modifications in the course of time. What is today taken for granted becomes the burning issue of tomorrow. These changes in our conceptions of justice can in one aspect be viewed as emerging from a competition among men for supremacy. The theory that the prevailing morality is in part set by dominating personalities and groups, and that this morality serves in part to advance the interests of those who are in a position to create it, is a hypothesis too probable to be rejected out of hand. But the reality here is complex, and the changes which occur in our moral attitudes may represent, in another aspect, the result of a competition among ideas, in which the success of a particular idea in getting itself realized in the affairs of men depends not upon its being taken up by the right people, but upon its intrinsic appeal, upon its reasonableness, upon its capacity to effect a happy compromise of conflicting human desires and thus found the basis for a satisfactory common life.

To my mind nothing is more preposterous than

LECTURE III

Kelsen's argument that natural law is inherently static, while his own view is dynamic.[7] He argues that natural law is static because it derives the legal order, not from a vacant principle of constitutionalism, but from certain meaningful notions of justice. These notions, he asserts, hold the legal order within a frame and freeze it into rigidity. This view simply ignores the plain fact that ideas are capable of growth, and that there is a process by which the common law, to use Mansfield's magnificent phrase, "works itself pure." If one wishes to be mystic one may describe this process in Hegelian terms as the dialectic of history. But in the end it remains as obvious, and as mysterious, as the process by which an anecdote changes and generally improves in the course of being retold. As for the alleged "dynamic" quality of Kelsen's own view, it seems to me to be about as "dynamic" as an empty wheelbarrow. To be sure, you can dump anything you wish into it, and you can push it

7 Die philosophischen Grundlagen der Naturrechtslehre und des Rechtspositivismus (1928) 19; *Die Idee des Naturrechts* (1927) 7 Zeitschrift für öffentliches Recht 221, 231; *Naturrecht und positives Recht* (1927) 2 Revue Internationale de la Théorie du Droit 71, 72.

in any direction you like. But there is absolutely
nothing to make it go.

The important practical question which emerges
from this discussion is not whether men are governed by ideas, for it is apparent that in part they
are, but whether this form of government ought to
be extended. Should we seek to bring human relations increasingly within the field of autonomous
and non-governmental control, or should our object be to reduce those relations to neat hierarchic
patterns, in which every man instead of being, as
Hobbes feared, wolf to another, becomes officer
to another? Certainly it would seem that the present is a time to broaden the field of autonomous
order. We live in a period when major readjustments in our economic and social order have become necessary. These readjustments inevitably
involve a shift in the constellations of power within
society. "The system" cannot be changed without
changing the relative positions of those who run
the system, and when you begin to shift men about
you produce friction, resentment, and humiliation.
Since many of these necessary changes have to be
brought about by legislative and administrative
decree, the power of governmental fiat is being

stretched to the utmost. Hobbes' plea for the sovereign power as the cornerstone of peace and order can hardly be expected to make a strong appeal at a time when the sovereign's most conspicuous activity consists in redistributing wealth. It would seem that the present is a time when our social structure requires to be held together by a cement firmer than that supplied by the abstract principle of respect for law as such. If Renan was right in assuming that men have the capacity for developing the illusions necessary for their survival, we ought to be seeing a revival of natural law. Though such a revival has often been heralded,[8] and though there are distinct signs of it in the law of the cases,[9] there is precious little

[8] See POUND, THE FORMATIVE ERA OF AMERICAN LAW (1938) 12, 93, and the references in note 33, p. 34, of the same work; Levi, *Natural Law, Precedent and Thurman Arnold* (1938) 24 VA. L. REV. 587. See also HAINES, THE REVIVAL OF NATURAL LAW CONCEPTS (1930); and CHARMONT, LA RENAISSANCE DU DROIT NATUREL (2d ed. 1927).

[9] Among many possible illustrations of this trend one may cite the extent to which courts have been undeterred by "the existing law of contracts" in protecting jobbers and retail dealers against an arbitrary termination of their agencies to sell specific products. See Fuller and Perdue, *The Reliance Interest in Contract Damages* (1937) 46 YALE L. J. 373, 415,

evidence that it has as yet substantially affected our law schools.

There are, I think, a number of factors which tend to explain why American legal scholarship has remained so unseasonably positivistic. There is, first of all, the enormous influence of Holmes. This influence has been particularly significant because it has most strongly affected those who by temperament would otherwise be most likely to contribute to the creation of a new common law. Nor has the effect of Holmes' example as a positivist been diminished by the circumstance that he did not always himself remain faithful to the program for a rigid separation of law and morals laid down in his early essays. The fact that he occasionally gave eloquent if somewhat vague expression to the human aspirations which prevent the law from ever being something which merely "is" actually

---

notes 217-218. A similar willingness to recognize ethical values not incorporated in traditional theories of contract law is revealed in those cases in which the courts have refused to give effect to a promisor's express stipulation against legal liability in order to protect a promisee who seriously changed his position in reliance on the promise. See Fuller, *Williston on Contracts* (1939) 18 N. C. L. REV. 1, 6, n. 9.

served, I believe, to reinforce the influence of his positivism by giving it an appearance of breadth and philosophic grounding. His very inconsistencies made him a more effective advocate of the positivistic philosophy than such men as Austin and Kelsen, who never let the green fields of life lure them from the gray path of logic.

Modern legal positivism also owes a great deal to the popularity of what is called the "scientific method." The current enthusiasm for this method has, I believe, led to the neglect of a rather obvious truth, which is that the question of the proper method for solving a problem depends to a large degree on the kind of problem to be solved. For example, the type of factual inquiry appropriate to determining whether our trains actually run on time is not necessarily the best way of finding out what we ought to do to make them run on time. A negative attitude which insists that judgment be suspended in the absence of controlled experiments or statistical demonstration is appropriate in many kinds of research. But to project this attitude over the whole field of law and ethics is to erect a substantial taboo against any intelligent discussion of the vague and shifting forces which ultimately shape men's lives.[10] When the "scientific method" is thus pervasively applied, the net effect is to render most "scientific" that theory which has the least to say—a circumstance from which legal positivism has drawn a large advantage in recent years.

Another factor explaining the continued vogue of the positivistic philosophy may be found in the resentment which has been aroused, at least in certain quarters, by the Supreme Court's rather too generous use of its power to veto legislation.[11] The decisions in which this power was exercised purported to rest, as a matter of fact, not on "natural reason" or anything equivalent to it, but on a body of positive law defining the competence of the legislative branch. The absence of any substantial warrant in the constitution itself for much of this assumed body of law, however, led naturally to the charge that the Supreme Court was applying "natural law," which meant in this case noth-

[10] Gény speaks somewhere of a modern *snobisme scientifique* which inhibits the exercise of common sense.

[11] I have in mind here the decisions of the Supreme Court of the United States during the past two or three decades.

ing more than that the court was making up its own law to suit itself. The opprobrious application of the term, in this connection tended, of course, to reinforce the already existing prejudice against anything which could be described as "natural law," and strengthened the feeling that the adoption of a passive and positivistic attitude toward the law as a whole was the only course consistent with complete intellectual integrity.

A final factor supporting the positivitistic attitude toward law is to be found, I believe, in the influence of a peculiarly modern conception of democracy. The force of this conception is not diminished, but rather increased, by the fact that it is not generally reduced to articulate expression. Here again it is Kelsen[12] who has been willing to trace out and accept the logical implications of an idea which most men are content to leave on the periphery of consciousness, where its full implica-

12 Vom Wesen und Wert der Demokratie (2d ed. 1929). See also his Staatsform und Weltanschauung (1933). Though Radbruch's defense of democracy (in his Rechtsphilosophie, 2d ed.) is based on a philosophy of relativism, his argument lacks the uncompromising "either—or" quality which characterizes Kelsen's thinking.

tions are held in check by competing notions and sentiments. The conception to which I refer is that which finds the justification for democracy in intellectual skepticism. There is no such thing as justice. Human reason is utterly incapable of regulating the relations of men among themselves. Some purely arbitrary principle of order becomes, therefore, necessary. Since power rests ultimately on the acquiescence of the governed, the most logical principle of government is that of majority rule, since this offers the broadest base for the order set up. It must be noted how purely negative this conception of democracy is. It does not adopt the common will from any notion that it is closer to the inner essence of things than the will of any particular individual. Majority rule is preferred not because it is most likely to be right, but because it is most likely to be obeyed. Democracy is rested not on an affirmation, but on a denial that government and law can in the end be anything but arbitrary.

In my opinion this attempt to found democracy on a negation would be dangerous in any age. It becomes positively suicidal at a time like the present, when major readjustments in the basic social

and economic structure of society are taking place.
This negative conception of democracy played an
important part, I am convinced, in bringing Germany and Spain to the disasters which engulfed
those countries. It was only this conception which
could mislead men into believing that the power
relations inside a society could be radically dis-
placed by the mere will of a numerical majority,
or that a social and economic revolution could be
accomplished through a democratic control un-
sustained by any common faith or program. It
was this conception which lulled men into the
dangerous dream that a kind of political euthanasia
of vested interests would be possible. In the rude
awakening which followed this dream there was
demonstrated, at least in Germany, not only the
futility of the dream itself, but the inability of
repressive violence to fill the void left by a de-
faulting principle of majority rule, for the purported counter-revolution of Nazism has in many
cases only increased the tempo and violence of the
disintegrative forces from which it claimed to be
rescuing Germany.

In my opinion, democracy must be founded not
on a negation of the force of ideas, but on a faith

that in the long run ideas are more important than the men who form them. The greatness of what we call democratic government does not lie in the mere fact that a numerical majority controls at election time, but at a point further removed from the ballot box, in the forces which are permitted to play upon the electorate. For in the world as it is now constituted, it is only in a democratic and constitutionally organized state that ideas have a chance to make their influence felt. By preserving a fluidity in the power structures of society, by making possible the peaceful liquidation of unsuccessful governments, democracy creates a field in which ideas may effectively compete with one another for the possession of men's minds. In a dictatorship, on the other hand, the chief requisite for the success of an idea is that it serve the interests of those who have enough power to make it effective. This is an inherent characteristic of dictatorships, though insight into this fact has been obscured, at least until recently, by the assumption that the totalitarian regimes were "ideological" in character.

I know of no more ironic demonstration of the impotence of ideas in a totalitarian regime than

that furnished by the experiences of a prominent
Austrian economist in Nazi Germany. This
scholar had for years been advocating economic
theories basically similar to those which formed a
part of the Nazi program. After the revolution
occurred in Germany, he naturally—though it now
seems, naively—assumed that since his ideas had
arrived in that country he had arrived with them.
Accordingly, he undertook a kind of triumphal
tour, scheduling lectures at most of the leading
German universities. He was received very coldly,
and was, I understand, finally denied altogether
the privilege of speaking. Why in a country presumably controlled by an "ideology" should this
treatment be accorded one who was so obviously of
the faith? The answer can best be stated in the
form of another question. Why should those who
had risked their lives and reputations to achieve
power move over to make room for a newcomer
simply because of the accident that he happened
to think the way they did? Ideas can play a
significant role only in countries where an aristo-
cratic government is so firmly entrenched that it
fears no revolution—a situation which probably
does not obtain anywhere today—or in countries

in which the succession of men in office is a familiar phenomenon and is accomplished without violence or excessive humiliation for those who must yield their positions. Where men's primary concern is with seizing and holding power, ideas inevitably become weapons in a struggle for position. Some years after the incident I have related, I read a very learned article in a German journal which demonstrated why the theories of the scholar in question had not been received by National Socialist economic science. It now appears that while they bore a superficial resemblance to the conceptions of National Socialism, they contained certain latent traces of Catholicism which made them unacceptable to the true believer in *Blut und Ehre*. Thus, to paraphrase Frederick the Great, does the scholar perform his function of furnishing an intellectual justification for the conquests of the bayonet and the loudspeaker.

The conception which finds the justification for democracy in skepticism is not only demonstrably incapable of sustaining a nation in time of crisis, but it has also, I believe, accelerated the disintegrative forces which threaten modern society. It has an inevitable tendency to inhibit the growth

125

of what I have called autonomous order by estopping those who might have contributed to that growth. If it is true that reason has nothing to say about man's relation to his fellows, then those who purport to speak in the name of reason are of course only using "reason" as a screen behind which to feather their own nests. The notion that all "ideologies" are mere cloaks for the interests of special groups has become a familiar one and it imposes a taboo the strength of which has been felt by many, I am sure, during the last ten years.

It is my belief that our society will not survive unless we can break through this taboo, unless we can reattain an atmosphere in which a man can gain a respectful audience for his views on the institution of private property in spite of the fact that he happens to own a house and lot. This atmosphere will only be regained when we have again come to believe that reason can have something to say concerning legal and social institutions. Some minimum faith in ideas is necessary to give practical significance to the doctrine of free speech and free thought. Only when this faith is re-established will the field of autonomous order be able to expand. Only in this way can major readjustments in our social structure be accomplished peaceably. Only so can our ideologies be brought into harmony with the needs of our times. You may, if you wish to be cynical, describe this as a proposal to cooperate with the inevitable by giving it a philosophy. You may with Ripert describe the proposal to revive natural law as involving merely a restoration to the scholar and thinker of his share in the rule of men over men.[13] To my mind neither of these ways of phrasing the issue in any way detracts from the necessity for escaping from the restraints which result from the still current prejudice against anything resembling natural law. These restraints will only be overcome, I believe, through the courage of individuals, and this means the courage not only to address an unfriendly audience, but also to overcome an inner aversion to what may look like a claim to oracular powers. Strong as this aversion may be, the scholar should

[13] "Lorsque M. Gény a fait de façon décisive le procès de l'interprétation scolastique du droit, il a été le grand défenseur de la puissance intellectuelle. Il a montré aux juristes comment ils pouvaient être des gouvernants." Ripert, *Droit Naturel et Positivisme Juridique* (1918), ANNALES DE LA FACULTÉ DE DROIT D'AIX, NOUVELLE SÉRIE, No. 1, p. 45.

remember that while he hesitates to assume a role bearing too unsavory a resemblance to that of the priest in primitive society the time may come when that role is no longer open to him, for we must recall that when the priest abdicates it is generally the warrior and spellbinder who take over.

Throughout these lectures I have been assuming that American legal scholarship suffers at present from the inhibitive effects of a positivistic philosophy. I cannot claim to have proved this thesis, nor shall I attempt to do so now. The tacit taboos imposed by a general climate of opinion are, after all, scarcely susceptible of demonstration, and I shall have to leave it to the informed reader to decide whether I have correctly sensed the prevailing bent of men's minds. Before closing, however, I should like to discuss briefly several specific ways in which the positivistic philosophy seems to me to work its effects on our legal thinking. These I mention not so much because I think they offer proof of my thesis, as because they will serve to make clearer what my thesis is and what it is I am objecting to when I condemn the positivistic philosophy.

Any appraisal of the prevailing temper of legal

thinking in this country would do well to take into account the notes on recent cases published in our law reviews. These unpretentious contributions to legal scholarship are for two reasons, I think, especially significant. In the first place, in them editorial restraint reduces individual creative effort to a minimum and they are in fact often the joint product of several minds. Accordingly, they represent a kind of cross section of the working philosophy of our law schools. In the second place, they touch the law of the cases at a vital spot, that is, where it is growing. The cases preferred are those involving situations putting a strain on existing legal doctrine; there is a tendency to choose decisions which from the standpoint of traditional theory seem "wrong." Though of course the notes vary in their content and approach, if one were to attempt to trace the pattern of the typical comment I think it would run something as follows. The author begins by pointing out the untenability of the explanations offered by the court for its decision. Though the court talked in the language of estoppel, it is impossible to make out the elements of a true estoppel in the facts of the case.

LECTURE III

An alternative ground of decision is equally un-
tenable. The writer concludes by remarking that
the court was no doubt impelled by extra-legal
considerations to depart from the strict letter of
legal theory. Sometimes this departure is approved;
sometimes it is not. Perhaps it is more commonly
approved today than formerly. But whether it is
approved or not, one thing is nearly certain. The
"extra-legal considerations" which prompted it will
not be discussed. Though these considerations
admittedly shape and control the judicial process,
they are still not a proper subject for discussion
in a law review. If this attitude is maintained, we
may in the next twenty years or so arrive at a point
where most of the living law of the cases will have
become "extra-legal" and "the law" itself will be
found only in the law schools. Obviously what is
needed is an enlargement of our conceptions of
what is legally relevant, though this step will cause
pain to the positivist since it will inevitably tend
to obscure the boundary between law and morality
and to import into the law the looser and freer
ways characteristic of ethical thinking.[14]

[14] Though I suggested in my article *American Legal Realism*

POSITIVISM AND LEGISLATIVE REFORM

A tacitly accepted philosophy of positivism seems to me also to underlie the modern preference for legislation as a means of legal reform. How often do we learn from the lips of even our most progressive judges and writers that "the remedy is with the legislature." Positivism has a natural tendency to prefer reform through legislation to that effected through the judicial process. The reason is obvious enough in the case of those forms of positivism which involve the conception of a sovereign power. Statute law is the kind of law which fits most readily into their theory; it is law in a form which introduces into the system no such internal stresses as those which are solved with such patent artificiality by the notion that what the sovereign permits he impliedly commands. But even those varieties of positivism which dispense with the notion of the sovereign have a natural affinity for the legislative process, for two related reasons.

(1934) 82 U. OF PA. L. REV. 429, 431-438, that one of the principal services of the realist movement in this country has been to enlarge the area of the "legally relevant," I do not believe that the prevailing philosophy of our law schools has as yet caught up with this broader conception of legal method.

Lecture III

In the first place, as I have attempted to show previously, all forms of legal positivism have the common characteristic of being *formal* in their method; they deal not with the content of the law but with its form and sanction. The positivists get so in the habit of thinking of the law as an empty container that they run the risk of forgetting that it is, after all, a body of living material.[15] If the creation of new law actually involved putting something into an empty container—as the positivist's habitual abstractive method inclines him to suppose—it would naturally be accomplished by legislation. Indeed, we would have no other word to describe the process, whether it was accomplished by a judge or a deliberative assembly.

In the second place, the common objective of all systems of positivism is to preserve a distinction between the law that is and the law that should be or is trying to be. Now legislation is the only kind of legal reform which does not threaten that distinction since legislation is reform which an-

---

[15] Maine finds the explanation for the historical affinity of utilitarianism and the theory of sovereignty in the abstractive method which both employ. EARLY HISTORY OF INSTITU-TIONS (1888) 398.

nounces itself as such. Judicial reform has a way of creeping up on us, and at any given point it is difficult to say whether the court is announcing a new rule or only making explicit assumptions which lay implicit in the old rule. This procedure is one which is naturally discomforting to the positivist, since it embarrasses the attainment of the main objective he seeks.

I know that the preference for reform through legislation is generally rested on grounds other than those I have mentioned. I am familiar with the arguments against reform through the judicial process. Our courts cannot act preventively, and often only get around to locking the stable door after the horse is stolen; they generally legislate in the worst possible way, that is, *ex post facto;* they will not assume the initiative, our judges being, as Menger expressed it, like defective clockworks which have to be shaken to set them going; finally, it takes money to set them going, and this means that they will not be set going at all unless someone has a sufficient interest at stake to justify him in risking the costs of a law suit. Yet with all these deficiencies, the judicial process has one enormous advantage over legislation in that its

133

decrees pass over readily into what I have called
the realm of autonomous order. The common law
imperceptibly becomes a part of men's common beliefs, and exercises a frictionless control over their
activities which derives its sanction not from its
source but from a conviction of its essential rightness.

One may agree with Thurman Arnold that the
greater moral persuasiveness of judge-made law is
not due entirely to its greater justice or efficiency,
but perhaps derives chiefly from the fact that a certain ritualistic aura softens and makes palatable
the realities of government by the judiciary.[16] But
it is difficult to agree with Mr. Arnold, or even to
understand him, when he passes from this observation to the conclusion that those who oppose other
forms of government, particularly that by bureau-
crats, are merely stupid. If bureaucracy is a form
of government which does not "go down well"
with those who have to be governed, then this seems
to me to constitute a legitimate argument against
that form of government and a reason for restrict-

16 THE SYMBOLS OF GOVERNMENT (1935); THE FOLKLORE OF
CAPITALISM (1937).

ing it to the unavoidable minimum. Particularly at a time when the exigencies of a prolonged economic depression have already strained the moral force of governmental fiat is there reason to prefer that form of government which controls moral attitudes less abstract than mere respect for the will of the state, and that means, I believe, preeminently government by judges.

It has been the service of a vigorous Swedish school of legal thought to bring home to us a realization of the extent to which the law, particularly judge-made law, shapes common morality.[17] They have shown us how false is the common picture according to which there exists outside the law, and wholly independent of it, a body of moral precepts which exerts a kind of one-way gravita-

[17] See OLIVECRONA, LAW AS FACT (1939) ; LUNDSTEDT, SUPERSTITION OR RATIONALITY IN ACTION FOR PEACE? (1925) ; LUNDSTEDT, DIE UNWISSENSCHAFTLICHKEIT DER RECHTSWISSENSCHAFT (1932). The leader of this school is Alex Hägerström, whose principal works are unfortunately available only in Swedish.

In connection with the point made in the text, it is interesting to compare the observations of Timasheff in AN INTRODUCTION TO THE SOCIOLOGY OF LAW (1939) 132, n. 17, concerning the effect of Soviet legal reforms on Russian conceptions of morality.

tional pull on the law, against which the law opposes a constant inertia, so that it lags always behind morality and only meets those minimum ethical demands which relate to the most pressing social needs. This whole "extra-legal" body of moral precepts is to a large extent a creature compounded of paper and ink and philosophic imagination. Actually, if we look to those rules of morality which have enough teeth in them to act as serious deterrents to men's pursuit of their selfish interests, we will find that far from being "extra-legal" they are intimately and organically connected with the functionings of the legal order. I may think that I drive carefully because it is my moral duty to do so as a good citizen, and I may suppose that the law merely takes over my standard of driving—which is, of course, that of the prudent man—as a test to apply to drivers less virtuous than myself. I forget to what extent my conceptions of my duty as a driver have been shaped by the daily activities of the traffic police. I forget that behind my standard of driving there may lie a vague fear of the ignominy involved in having to appear in traffic court, and that this fear may have had a great deal to do with shaping my conceptions of traffic morality.

It should be noted that the view I am expounding here does not assert that men are, in the ordinary affairs of life, consciously deterred by legal penalties. It concedes that the effective deterrents which shape the average man's conduct derive from morality, from a sense of right and wrong. What it asserts is that these conceptions of right and wrong are themselves significantly shaped by the daily functionings of the legal order, and that they would be profoundly altered if this legal order were to disappear. As business men we may perform our contracts not because we are afraid of a law suit, but because we feel that it is our duty to do so. But would this same conception of duty exist if the law enforced no contracts at all? In the moral environment out of which this conception of duty arises, is not the law itself one of the most important elements?

The judge in deciding cases is not merely laying down a system of minimum restraints designed to keep the bad man in check, but is in fact helping to create a body of common morality which will define the good man. When he sees his office in this light, the judge will realize, I think, how significantly creative his work is, and how sinister is the temptation to evade his responsibilities to the future by adopting a passive and positivistic attitude toward "the existing law."

As a final inhibitive influence of positivism I should like to mention the effect which it has on that kind of legal scholarship which expresses itself in the writing of treatises and technical articles. Here the most repressive effect of the positivistic philosophy lies, I believe, in the fear it engenders of a very simple question. Everyone who has attempted to write on the law of the cases must have been concerned by the possibility that his readers might pose this question to him: "Does this article state the law, or only your idea of what the law ought to be?" Positivism demands that this question be answered, for obviously if it cannot then the basic distinction which positivism seeks to preserve is lost. Yet the writer may feel great embarrassment in answering it. To say that he is stating the law as it is will seem to involve either a species of fraud or a kind of omniscience which he has no intention of claiming. On the other hand, he does not like to say that he is only offering for consideration a series of personal reactions to the law, for he may well feel that he has, to a degree not precisely ascertainable, only made explicit ideas which were already implicit in the cases.

Caught in this dilemma, the scholar may decide not to write at all. Or he may devote himself to problems of methodology, discussing the proper approach to law without incurring the responsibility for applying it. Or he may adopt a style so obscure that it is impossible to tell exactly what objective he seeks, and hence impossible to criticize him for having evaded his duties to positivism. That all of these things are occurring is abundantly evidenced in our law reviews.

How repressive is this demand that the legal scholar ticket precisely his own contribution can be seen if we imagine a similar demand to be made in fields outside the law. Suppose the worker in a scientific laboratory were forbidden to announce a discovery unless he were able to say precisely how much of it represented his own work and how much that of his predecessors and colleagues? Suppose the surgeon were forbidden to operate unless he could tell of each movement of his scalpel whether it was intended to restore the organism to the condition it was in before being stricken with disease or to bring about a new condition of the organism which would enable it to survive? Suppose the artist were forbidden to paint a picture unless he could say of each stroke of his brush whether it was a true representation of nature or an imaginative interpretation of his own? No science or art could long survive such a limitation. I see no reason to think that the law is different. I have never found anyone who would not admit that there is an element of creation and discovery in the law. It seems to me as clear as anything can be that the positivistic philosophy in its usual forms tends to stifle this element.

The judge or legal writer ought not to be ashamed of his inability to answer the question which positivism puts to him. Rather, he ought to be proud that his contribution is such that it cannot be said with certainty whether it is something new or only the better telling of an old story. This is the best possible guaranty that his work is at once creative and sound, and that he is playing his part in the eternal process by which the common law works itself pure and adapts itself to the needs of a new day.

Index

INDEX

Ahrens, 102.
Analytical jurisprudence, 27-41; compared to theology, 80-81.
   See also Austin, gaps in the law, Somló, and sovereignty.
Aquinas, 101.
Arnold, 134.
Austin, his theory of sovereignty, 26-41; contradictions of his
   theory, 46; 84; 88; 89; 91; 103.
Autonomous order, 110-114; 125-128.

Behaviorism and legal realism, 55-57.
Bergbohm, 17; 18; 23; 27; 31-32; 39.
Bingham, 52.
Bodin, 19-20.

Cardozo, 62.
Cavers, 66.
Charmont, 116.
Cohen, 7; 63; 108.
Comte, 17.
Contradictory laws, 37.
Cook, 40; 50; 52; 53; 54; 63-64.
Custom, relation between, and theory of sovereignty, 31-32,
   80.

Del Vecchio, 23; 31.
Democracy, Kelsen's conception of, 120-121; role of ideas in a,
   122-125.
Dickinson, 75-76.
Duguit, 17.
Durkheim, 17.

The Julius Rosenthal Foundation
For General Law

JULIUS ROSENTHAL, an eminent and beloved member of the Chicago bar, was born in Germany on September 17, 1828. He pursued his studies at the Universities of Heidelberg and Freiburg, came to Chicago in July, 1854, and was admitted to the bar in 1860. He was especially prominent as a practitioner in the law of wills and in probate and real estate law. As librarian of the Chicago Law Institute from 1867 to 1877 and again from 1888 to 1903, and its president from 1878 to 1880, he was chiefly responsible for its development. He was a member of the first Board of State Law Examiners of Illinois, and its secretary (1897-1899). He died May 14, 1905.

Julius Rosenthal was a lawyer of great learning and rare scholarly attainments. He labored long and earnestly to establish the best standards of legal scholarship. His interest in the welfare of the Law School of Northwestern University was constantly manifested, and of this his numerous gifts of books were tokens.

To honor his memory the University in 1919 established The Julius Rosenthal Foundation for General Law. The income derived from the Foundation is, among other uses, applicable to the cultivation of legal literature, and particularly to the publication of meritorious essays, monographs, and books of a scientific or practical nature concerning the law; to the aid or encouragement of research in the field of legal literature and the preparation for publication of the results of such research; and to the delivery and publication of lectures on subjects concerning the law.

www.ingramcontent.com/pod-product-compliance
Lightning Source LLC
Chambersburg PA
CBHW031548260326
41914CB00002B/323

*9 7 8 1 5 8 4 7 7 0 1 6 9 *